**A Brief Encounter
By Susan A. York**

Walk With Grace Publishing, LLC 2644
2016

Copyright © 2016 by Susan A. York
All rights reserved

ISBN—9 780692032275

Library of Congress Control Number: LLC 2644

Book design and illustrations by Susan A. York

Printed in the United States of America

ABOUT THE BOOK

The book "A Brief Encounter" is a true story, a crime story, and a love story.

The crime took place at Cripple Creek, Colorado in 1994. Paul, the main character in the book, grows a considerable amount of marijuana. The police confiscate 120 pounds of marijuana. At the same time, Paul is a city building inspector.

Paul was sentenced to twenty-six months in prison. He served his time in prison, first going to the intake center at Colorado Territorial Correctional Facility in Canon City, Colorado, then to Colorado State Penitentiary in Canon City, Colorado and then to Arrowhead Correctional Facility in Canon City, Colorado.

In 1996, he was transferred to Colorado State Penitentiary, a minimum security prison in Canon City, Colorado. He entered the Alcohol and Drug Treatment Program in March of 1996.

ABOUT THE AUTHOR

Susan A. York lives in Baker City, Oregon. She has lived there since 1988.

Susan is a member of a writing group that meets once a week at the Baker County Public Library.

Susan was inspired by Eloise Dielman, her writing teacher of the writing group to complete her book, "A Brief Encounter." Eloise, prior to her death in 2015, said to Susan, "You need to finish that story." The book took twenty years to complete. With patience and perseverance, Susan completed the book in 2016.

In addition to being a writer, Susan is an award-winning photographer. She has a photograph on permanent exhibit in Sapporo, Japan. The title of the photograph is, "A Gathering of Geese." She only found out later that the goose is a lucky sign of the Japanese...

FROM THE AUTHOR

I wrote this book to capture the essence of a person who commits a crime, and who eventually serves time in prison.

The narrative describes how two total strangers form an intimate and compelling relationship.

TABLE OF CONTENTS

DEDICATION

The story, "A Brief Encounter" by Susan A. York, is dedicated to Eloise Dielman who encouraged Susan to complete/finish her story prior to her death in 2015. The 3rd writing group that meets every week at the Baker County Public Library. Susan attended for a short time during 2011 and 2015.*

Eloise was a longtime friend of the Baker County Public Library and was known as a giving member of the Baker County community. She died in 2015 at the age of 75 years old. She encouraged many writers to write about anything as long as they wrote something.

The subjects could vary: cats, dogs, family memories, history, such as World War II...

Without Eloise's love for writing, writers in the writing group wouldn't have benefited from her devotion.

ACKNOWLDEGEMENTS

Persons Assisting with Research on the Book

Elizabeth Peterson
University of Oregon

Obtained a researcher for myself. His name is William G. Wittenbrock.

Maggie Wollaston
Human Resources Operations Administration
Dept. of Corrections
State of Oregon

Mary Rumsey
Reference and Instructional Services Librarian
Willamette University
College of Law

Jeffrey Robel
U.S. Dept. of Commerce
National Oceanic and Atmospheric Administration
National Environmental Satellite Data and Information Service
National Climatic Data Center
Asheville, NC

Joan Campf
First writing teacher at Lake Oswego Senior High School
Lake Oswego, Oregon

Sylvia Bowers
Staff person at the Baker County Public Library in Baker City, Oregon, who gave countless hours of her time in doing research for the book for Susan.

Perry F. Stokes
Library Director, Adams County Public Library
Baker City, Oregon

The Entire staff at Baker County Public Library, Baker City, Oregon

Kyra L. Reddington, Typist/ Publisher's Assistant

KC Wilson- Cover Image from Duggal's

Kim Hilburn- Blog Developer

The Oregonian—Archival Information

The World—Archival Information
The Cripple Creek Valley Sentinel—Archival Information

Adams County Circuit Court, Coquille, Oregon

Adams County Sheriff's Office, Coquille, Oregon

Multnomah County Public Library

Central Branch, Information Services, Portland, Oregon

Kelly J. Officer, Criminal Justice Commission, Salem, Oregon

Debbie Harmon, KATU Television Station, Portland, Oregon

A STATEMENT FROM THE AUTHOR

Having been a state certified alcohol and drug counselor, I have ethical standards to follow. The most important ethical standard is to do no harm to a client.

In counseling, it is a process to establish a relationship and create a dialogue between counselor and client. It takes a considerable amount of time and work with care and concern. It is something that just doesn't happen overnight. You have to build trust with that person, that person you are attempting to help.

I wish to take this opportunity to express with regret to Paul and those other persons that may have been affected by my actions and eventual leaving of a position that I thoroughly loved and enjoyed.

I pray that no long term damage was done.

AFTERWORD

Susan A. York's original manuscript was written in long hand from 1996 to 2016. The text and storyline was started during the fall of 1996.

PARABLE

"God is able to make all Grace Abound Toward You…"

II Corinthians 9:8

Chapter 1

The Crime

A BRIEF ENCOUNTER

It was an ordinary Monday, on October 5, 1994. Sergeant Zanni from the Cripple Creek Sheriff's Office, was walking Percy. Percy had confiscated $800,000 worth of drugs in his lifetime. Sergeant Zanni was Percy's handler. As they were walking in downtown Cripple Creek, they were running some errands during their lunch hour.

Percy, all of a sudden received a positive hit. A gentleman was walking in the opposite direction across the street from them. He had deposited his paycheck for $2395.00, his salary for 8 days of work as a city building inspector.

Paul pulled out of the parking lot of U.S. National Bank heading toward and past the pole building at 2755 Shelly Road, one mile east of Cripple Creek, Colorado. He would be traveling today to the office in Cripple Creek. Tomorrow, he would be in Gold Mine. He was a city building inspector for the cities of Cripple Creek and Gold Mine, Colorado. He worked two days a week. It was only a minute drive from Cripple Creek to Shelly Road.

The fall landscape in the year of 1994 was especially beautiful with shades of glimmering amber, orange and red leaves in the surrounding trees which dotted the hills around Cripple Creek.

Unfortunately, all the timber mills had been shut down and people found themselves employed either in government or the tourist industry.

The property Paul owned included ten acres and gave a certain amount of privacy, but it was close enough to the town of Cripple Creek.

Before he left, he had told Teresa, his wife, to go pay their bill at Cripple Creek Supply, a local hardware store. They owed $2,400.00. He carefully counted out the money in hundred dollar bills. Even though Teresa didn't have a driver's license, she had her orders from Paul to pay the bill that day.

The bills had piled up for the grow operation. Paul had even called upon Steven and Peter to help with the grow operation. They were going to help out in harvesting the marijuana. They had traveled from Monterey and Oxnard, California. Both Steven and Peter were avid surfers.

Teresa left Shelly Road headed for Cripple Creek Supply. She carried the money in her handbag. Cripple Creek Supply had everything from ceiling fans, ladders, shop vacuums, table saws and weight scales. Everything Paul needed for the grow operation.

A young man was waiting at the counter as Teresa entered the building. Teresa took out the money from her handbag and told the young man she would be paying the entire bill. The account was in her name. She handed over the money to the clerk. He carefully counted out the money, thinking it was strange that someone would pay in one hundred dollar bills. Then he handed her a receipt for the payment.

After Teresa left the store, Sergeant Zanni, from the Cripple Creek's Sheriff Office, talked to Curtis Jack, the manager for Cripple Creek Supply. The clerk smelled something suspicious. The date was October 7, 1994.

Sergeant Zanni was a good officer who had in excess of sixteen years of police officer experience. He liked his job very much and was proud to serve his community. He was well respected throughout Cripple Creek.

After talking to Curtis Jack, Sergeant Zanni placed a call into him that afternoon to speak to him regarding narcotic tainted money. Mr. Jack voiced that he was very concerned about receiving $2,400 in $100 bills. Mr. Jack told Sergeant Zanni that on October 7, Teresa Patterson had come into Cripple Creek Supply and had paid for building materials with cash in the amount of $2,400, all in $100 bills. Mr. Jack told Sergeant Zanni, the money smelled "funny." Mr. Jack told Sergeant Zanni that Paul Patterson worked for the city of Cripple Creek and does not have an adequate income to make this amount of cash readily available. Mr. Jack also told Sergeant Zanni that employees of Cripple Creek Supply had delivered merchandise to the Patterson residence and that Mr. Patterson was always inside a pole building on his property. That, in order to contact Mr. Patterson, his wife, Teresa, had to contact Paul verbally and identify herself before Mr. Patterson would come out of the pole building, which was locked from the outside. Whenever Mr. Patterson exited the pole building, his actions were suspicious in that he exited in a manner to keep anyone from seeing inside.

Mr. Jack told Sergeant Zanni he personally knew Paul Patterson. Mr. Jack said Mr. Patterson resides in a camp trailer and is building a new house at 2755 Shelly Road. Mr. Jack told Sergeant Zanni that he has known Paul Patterson for about the last year.

IN THE DISTRICT COURT OF THE STATE OF COLORADO
FOR ADAMS COUNTY

FILED
1994 OCT 11 AM 11:13

ADAMS COUNTY COURT
CRIPPLE CREEK, COLORADO

STATE OF COLORADO,

Plaintiff,

vs

Paul Jonah Patterson

AKA's   **AFFIDAVIT FOR SEARCH WARRANT**

Paul Jonah Patterson

AKA's

Paul S. Patterson
Paul Jonah Paterson
Paul Jonah Peterson
Paul Jonah Pitterson
Paul Jonah Putterson

ET. AL.

Defendants.

STATE OF COLORADO	)	
	)	**ss**
County of Adams	)	

IN THE DISTRICT COURT OF THE STATE OF COLORADO
FOR ADAMS COUNTY

I, the undersigned, upon my oath do hereby depose and say, that I, Paul L. Foster, as a Detective with the Adams Police Department and I have been a Police Officer for over 5 years. My current assignment is as a member of the South River Interagency Narcotics Team. The area in which I work narcotics includes Adams, Morgan, and Arapahoe Counties in Colorado. During my tenure as a career Police Officer, I have had training and on the job experience in the investigation of numerous types of crimes which includes but is not limited to the investigation of narcotics violations, burglaries, and the various types of thefts which includes thefts by deception and thefts of services.

Further that during my tenure as a career Police Officer, I have used training and on the job experience in the investigation of narcotics and narcotic related crimes including methamphetamine, LSD, heroin, cocaine and marijuana. I have been trained to identify many controlled substances. This training included the methods of use, delivery, possession, and manufacture of said controlled substances.

I have had training from the Police certification process in Colorado. I have also had training from the Department of the Interior of the Federal Government, training sponsored by the Department of the Interior's Marijuana Eradication and Reconnaissance Team of which I was a member. Part of my training dealt with the conspiracy to possess, process, delivery, and manufacture controlled substances and how to investigate these types of crimes. I have used the techniques learned to investigate narcotic related crimes.

Part of my responsibilities include interviewing persons who are criminally involved in, have been criminally involved in, and/or are citizen informants trying to give Law Enforcement officers information about illegal narcotics activity. I have been trained on how to establish the reliability of persons giving information to Law Enforcement about illegal narcotics activity. Over 10 search warrants have been issued based on information provided by these informants and these warrants led to seizures of controlled substances, arrests and convictions of persons responsible for controlled substance violations.

During this training, I was trained to identify marijuana in all of its common forms and states of refinement. The training and professional experience of over 5 years of being a Police Officer has acquainted me with the tools and methods used to grow, possess, process, use and sell marijuana. I have been involved in over 50 seizures of marijuana growing operations including over 10 indoor growing operations in which marijuana was either started under grow lights or totally grown indoor growing type operations. That I know that persons who grow marijuana indoCOS often divert or attempt to conceal their high power consumption from law enforcement. This power diversion is usually completed by the marijuana growers themselves, without the benefit of the proper electrical and building permits having first being obtained. I have been investigating marijuana growing related crimes since 1988 and during this time I have been responsible for or involved in the seizure of many hundreds of marijuana plants. During the seizures I have quite often spoke with suspects in the cases and have essentially been educated by persons who were actively involved in the marijuana growing on how they in fact grew marijuana.

During my tenure as a Police Officer I have been involved in over 100 investigations involving theft and narcotic related offenses. I have been involved in the issuance of over 10 search warrants during these investigations. When the locations were searched, the warrants led to the seizure of controlled substances and related evidence along with stolen property.

This affidavit will show that Paul Jonah Patterson and Teresa Matthews Patterson and others are currently involved in the manufacture and conspiracy to manufacture marijuana at 2755 Shelly Road, Adams County, Colorado.

10-07-94 I met with Detective Sergeant Craig Zanni from the Sheriff's Office. Sgt. Zanni told me he has been a Police Officer in excess of 16 years. I have worked with Sgt. Zanni for the last 5 years and know him to be an honest and reliable person. On this date Sgt. Zanni told me the following information:

10-07-94 Sgt. Zanni had contacted Cripple Creek Supply manager Curtis Jack, who had requested to speak with him regarding narcotic tainted money. That Mr. Jack is a well-respected member in the community and was very concerned about receiving $2400.00 in cash, all in one hundred dollar bills. Mr. Jack told Sgt. Zanni that on 10-06-94 Teresa Patterson had come into Cripple Creek Supply and paid for the building materials with cash in the amount of $2400.00, all in $100.00 bills. Mr. Jack told Sgt. Zanni the money had been paid to an employee of Cripple Creek Supply and the employee had gone to Mr. Jack and shown him the cash. Mr. Jack told Sgt. Zanni the money smelled "funny". Mr. Jack told Sgt. Zanni that Paul Patterson works for the city of Cripple Creek and does not have an adequate income to make this amount of cash readily available. Mr. Jack also told Sgt. Zanni that employees of Cripple Creek Supply told Mr. Jack that when they had delivered merchandise to the Patterson's residence that Paul Patterson was inside a pole building on his property. That to contact Paul Patterson his wife, Teresa Patterson, had to contact him verbally and identify herself before Paul would come out of the pole building, which was locked from the inside. That when Paul exited the pole building, his actions were suspicious in that he exited in a manner to keep anyone from seeing inside.

On or about 10-10-94, Sgt. Zanni showed a photo of the Patterson property to the employee of Cripple Creek Supply who had been to the Patterson property. This is the same photo later described in this affidavit as being taken by Detective Looney of SRINT of the Patterson property during a marijuana eradication flight. The employee positively identified the photo as the PATTERSON property.

Mr. Jack told Sgt. Zanni he personally knew Paul Patterson is currently the Cripple Creek/Gold Mine* city building inspector, who does reside in a camp type trailer and is building a new house at 2755 Shelly Road, Cripple Creek, Colorado. Mr. Jack told Sgt. Zanni that he has known Paul Patterson for about the last year.

Sgt. Zanni told me that on 10-07-94, he talked to Sgt. Carl Nayaert of the Gold Mine Police Department. Sgt. Nayaert told Sgt. Zanni that Paul Patterson makes a salary of $2395.00 per month. Sgt. Nayaert told Sgt. Zanni he had gotten this information from city records. I know that salaries of city employees ate a matter of public record.

That Sgt. Zanni then contacted Chief Knapp of the Cripple Creek Police Department. That Chief Knapp found in the city records that a Paul J. Patterson is a part-time city employee. Paul Patterson works as the city building inspector. His employment application lists a social security number of 570-96-4556, along with Colorado DL# of 5353226. This returns through DMV records to Patterson, Paul Jonah with a date of birth of 9-15-55.

Sgt. Zanni responded to Mr. Jack's place of business and had Mr. Jack hide the twenty four (24) one hundred dollar bills on the business property. After the money had been hidden, Sgt. Zanni allowed Percy (Adams County Narcotic Detection Canine) to walk through the business property area. Sgt. Zanni advised that as Percy walked through the area he alerted to the presence and location where the cash was hidden. Sgt. Zanni advised that this is a positive reaction the canine has to the presence of the odor of a narcotic which Percy has been trained to detect.

Sgt. Zanni told me that he has worked with Percy for more than six years. That he (Sgt. Zanni) is a certified State Master Trainer with the Colorado Police Canine Association and Percy is a certified Narcotic Detection Canine. That during this period, Percy has been responsible for more than fifty felony arrests and the seizures of more than $800,000.00 worth of narcotics.

On 10-07-94 I caused a check to be made with Pacific Power and Light in Adams and learned their records indicate the current residents of 2755 Shelly Road to be Paul and Teresa Patterson.

On or about 10-07-994, I cased a check to be made through the Colorado Department of Motor Vehicles and learned Paul Jonah Patterson's date-of-birth 09-15-55, holds a valid Colorado driver's license bearing number 5353226. Colorado DMV records also show Teresa Matthews Patterson's driver's license, however, a number has been issued to her, this number being 5563475. Colorado DMV shows the following vehicles registered to the Patterson's:

1983 Jeep, Colorado license/LUVMUD.
1988 Dodge 4-door, Colorado license/RNN983.
1993 Terry RT, Colorado license/R667724.

Further, on or about 10-07-94, a check was made through the Law Enforcement Data System (LEDS) and the National Crime Information Center (NCIC) and learned Paul Jonah Patterson's date-of-birth is 09-15-55 and he has been arrested numerous times in the past. These arrests were in New Mexico, they include the following:

1975 H&S—Plant/Cultivate/ETC Marijuana/Hash, Receive/ETC Known Stolen Property
1976 H&S—Possess Control Substance Paraphernalia
1976 VC—Take Vehicle W/O Owner Consent/ Vehicle Theft
1977 H&S—Possess Controlled Substance
1977 PC—Possess Drugs/Alcohol/ETC in Prison/Jail
1980 PC—Assault With Deadly Weapon, H&S—Plant/Cultivate/ETC Marijuana/Hash.

1983 H&S—Sell or Transport Marijuana/Hash, H&S—Posses Marijuana/Hashish For Sale, H&S—Keep Place to Sell/ETC Controlled Substance.

I noted on the criminal history of Paul Jonah Patterson that under his alias names, it appears Patterson changed the spelling of his last name in slight degrees. Alias names include the following:
Patterson, Jonah S.
Paterson, Paul Jonah
Peterson, Paul Jonah
Pitterson, Paul Jonah
Putterson, Paul Jonah

In my training and experience I know that people involved in illegal activity will often change the spelling of their names by adding or removing letters. This is done to confuse Law Enforcement and make it more difficult to locate the true name and criminal history of the suspect.

Further, I noted on the Adams County Assessor's record that Paul and Teresa spell their last name as Paterson. While on each of their Colorado Driving Records their last name is spelled as Patterson.

On October 8, 1994, Detective Dan Looney of SRINT was an observer in a helicopter during a marijuana eradication flight. Detective Looney is a Adams County Sheriff's Office Detective currently assigned to SRINT. Detective Looney has been a Police Officer in excess of 11 years. I know Detective Looney personally and know him to be an honest and reliable person. Detective Looney told me the helicopter he was in flew over the Patterson property and Detective Looney was able to take a photograph I have since seen the photograph and I noticed a large, blue shop or pole building. The building has an opaque roof made of what appears to be corrugated plastic. When looking at the photo I could see through the roof into the second story of the building and I could see what appears to be numerous green plants, similar in size and shape to green marijuana plants.

On or about 10-10-94, I drove by the Patterson property and also did observe the photograph taken by Detective Looney. I would describe it as follows: 2755 Shelly Road, Cripple Creek, Adams County, Colorado. To reach the property you would drive to Cripple Creek then drive west on 3nd Avenue from the Adams County Jail/Courthouse for approximately 1 and a half miles. As you reach the cross street of W. First Place, 3rd Avenue turns into Shelly Road. Approximately 1 mile from the Jail/Courthouse you will pass a Latter Day Saints Church, you will continue on for about a half mile further when you will see a silver mailbox on the right side of the roadway. The numbers "2755" are on this mailbox. About 20 feet behind this mailbox is a wooden sign which reads "2755 Shelly Road" and has an arrow pointing up the left fork of the road. You would then drive up the roadway in the direction the arrow indicated. About 50 feet from the fork in the roadway you would see a green metal gate which has a sign which reads "Private property". The initial approximate 15 feet of the driveway leading to 2755 is concrete. The buildings on the property include a large, blue, metal shop/ pole building with an opaque roof. There is a trailer on the property with a wooden shed attached to it. There is also a basement foundation that has been constructed for a residence. This is the Patterson property as described above.

That it is my experience that persons growing marijuana often start and store marijuana plants in buildings and their residence. Kept in these buildings are the implements to grow and cultivate marijuana, including but not limited to marijuana seeds which are necessary to start marijuana plants and are a by-product of marijuana processing, germinating marijuana seeds, small marijuana plants, growing light systems for starting marijuana plants and continuing indoor type grow operations, fertilizers, tools such as hoes, rakes, pruning shears, watering cans, and hoses, and other tools necessary to cultivate the controlled substance marijuana. Further marijuana cultivatCOS often keep records of plant growth, watering, and fertilizing in their residences and outbuildings.

I also know based on my training and experience that the indoor cultivation of marijuana is accomplished by persons utilizing high intensity lights, such as halide and sodium lights, transformers, timers, irrigation equipment, fans, pumps, CO_2 cylinders, vermiculate, soil, and pots, and other equipment. In addition the cultivatCOS often possess literature describing methods of cultivation, photographs of their crops, written records of cultivation, and written records of equipment purchases and drug sales. That it is necessary to seize this type of documentation to show persons that may be involved in the ongoing conspiracy and ongoing manufacture of the controlled substance marijuana.

In my experience I have also found that it is common for persons growing marijuana to harvest and prune the plants as a part of the growing process, and that they most frequently take this into their residence or outbuildings for processing or for early sales or personal use. Also as marijuana matures, it is most often taken into the building to be cured and prepared for sales and use.

Further, that in marijuana growing operations, there is a significant monetary investment to set up this type of operation. I therefore request to seize records of money spent or gained from this illegal operation, as well as large sums of money, which may have been obtained from this illegal operation, and may be present in the residence, outbuildings, or vehicles located at the location. [Large sums of money would range from a few hundred to many thousands of dollars. Further that people who manufacture and deal illegal narcotics conceal their money in safe deposit boxes, real estate, stocks, bonds, gold, silver, exotic animals, and many other types of investments.

That as an experienced narcotics investigator I have learned that persons involved in the use, possession, and sales of controlled substances often use the telephone to conduct their illegal operation.] That while serving search warrants at locations where controlled substance violations are occurring, that most frequently officers answer the telephone and the callers are asking for the defendants in the case. That other officers, and myself, have made arrangements to deliver controlled substances to callers during the subsequent conversations. That it is not uncommon for callers to be specific in their requests for controlled substance, and the quantity they want to purchase. Additionally that it is not uncommon for the same person to call back several times to complete a transaction, or seeking the defendants, and that this is an indication to me that the defendants are in the business of dealing controlled substances based on my experience and training. That as part of this affidavit that I would request permission to record incoming phone calls to the residence, and that these recording would be the best evidence in the crimes of conspiracy to deliver controlled substances, and the attempted possession of controlled substances. That these recordings would be available to the court in any criminal prosecution on the defense of entrapment, which I know to be a common defense of persons charged with these crimes.

Through training and experience, I also know that people who conspire to sell or who sell controlled substances often times will have attached to their telephones a phone answering device. This is done so that these people who are conspiring or selling controlled substances do not miss important messages from other co-conspirators or prospective buyers of their product. I know through experience that the tapes from these recording devise are often times important pieces of evidence to law enforcement to prove the crimes of conspiracy. That as part of this affidavit that I would request permission to seize these phone answering devices, and/or recordings from these phone answering devices.

I have learned through my training and experience that many times people who sell and deliver illegal narcotics are highly mobile and use their vehicle to facilitate their narcotics transactions. I have also learned that many times, evidence of these transactions are left in their vehicles. This evidence includes, but is not limited to, packaging material, records, controlled substances, and cash. Also I have learned that persons involved in the conspiracies to possess, distribute, and manufacture their controlled substances, often hide the evidence in their vehicle, so that they may have it with them during any narcotic transactions, or so that they may leave their residence in a hurry taking the evidence with them.

In addition people involved in controlled substance violations often use several vehicles, including those of friends and associates. They also purchase vehicles and fail to change the registration into their name. This is done to keep law enforcement from identifying assets they may own, and also keep law enforcement form being able to identify during drug deals.

Further that my training and experience in narcotics investigation has taught me that persons involved in the conspiracies to possess, distribute, and manufacture controlled substances do so over long periods of time. Further that these conspiracies are comprised of separate acts over a period of days, weeks, and months.

Further that evidence of the conspiracy/s remain after the actual act/s may have been completed. This evidence includes notes, correspondence, phone bills, receipts for items used in the conspiracy or in the furtherance of the conspiracy, equipment used in the conspiracy, proceeds of the conspiracy, and other items used in the conspiracy. That these items, as well as the controlled substances themselves, or evidence thereof, may be found weeks and months after the conspiracy has taken place.

That in my training and experience that I have learned that persons related in the crimes associated with possession, use, sales and manufacture of controlled substances keep about their persons, residences, and vehicles items known as evidence of domicile and control. These items include, but are not limited to, power and phone bills, photographs, bank records, personal identifications and correspondence, rent receipts, motel receipts, address books and phone numbers. These items are necessary to prove possession and ownership of the controlled substances and to assist in identifying conspirators in the conspiracies to possess, sell, and manufacture controlled substances.

That through my training and experience, I have learned that first names or nicknames listed on pieces of paper of small notebooks with what appear to be dollar amounts after them, are often times records of narcotics transactions, and money owed to the persons who has possession of these records, and that person who sell controlled substances illegally often keep such records on their person, and in their residence and vehicle. I also know that these records are often called "tally sheets", and are in fact business records of their illegal activity.

That through my training and experience I know that many times that people who use and distribute controlled substances often sell or trade stolen property for controlled substances. Furthermore I know that these people will often receive items such as but not limited to, televisions, VCR's, cameras, stereos, guns, and other household items, for controlled substances. People involved in controlled substance violations also accumulate items such as these as the proceeds and profits from their illegal drug activity.

That I have often found that persons who possess, and sell controlled substances, not only keep them in their residence, but often hide them in outbuildings and surroundings of their residence and I therefore request to search the area commonly known as the curtilage of the residence.

That further in my 5 years of experience, that I have learned that when a person(s) engage in the illegal possession, manufacture and use of controlled substances, that most frequently, and in almost all cases, more than one controlled substance is found in their residence or possession.

Based upon information provided by Sergeant Craig Zanni, Mr. Jack, and my investigation I have probably cause to believe and do believe that Paul J. Patterson, Teresa Patterson, and persons yet unknown who live and/or control the residence located at 2755

Shelly Road, Cripple Creek, Adams County, Colorado, are involved in the conspiracy to commit the felony crimes of the conspiracy to sell, deliver and manufacture the controlled substance marijuana. I also have probable cause to believe, and do believe that the above mentioned persons are in possession of controlled substances including growing marijuana, as well as other items used in the manufacture of controlled substances such as but not limited to marijuana, marijuana grow equipment including but not limited to halide lights, sodium lights, ballasts, generatCOS, 1000 watt bulbs and equipment to used controlled substances such as but not limited to packaging material, sales, plastic sandwich bags and smoking devices, as well as paper work and records of narcotics transactions, and sales such as list with names and dollar amounts, large sums of money which would be the profit from the sales of controlled substances, and other items as described above.

I therefore request a search warrant be issued authorizing a search of the premises, curtilage, and vehicles owned by, under the control of, or registered to the defendants as listed above for evidence of these crimes, and if any of them are found, authorizing seizure of the same.

SOUTH RIVER INTERAGENCY NARCOTICS TEAM
1975 MCPHERSON RM 302
DENVER, CO 97444
942-7813

PRESS RELEASE

CONTACT PERSON:
Kathy Smartt Analyst
Administrative Assistant
756-2020 Ext 559

DATE: THURSDAY October 13, 1994
TIME: 11:50 AM

SUBJECT: MARIJUANA GROW CONSPIRACY

WEDNESDAY October 12, 1994 at 0900

SRINT Team members assisted the Adams County Sheriff's Office, Cripple Creek and Gold Mine* Police Departments in execution of a search warrant as a residence located at 2755 Shelly Road, Cripple Creek, Adams County, Colorado. This is the residence of Paul and Teresa Patterson. Patterson was employed as a building inspector for the Cities of Cripple Creek and Gold Mine*.

Located at the residence upon arrival of the agents were Peter Oliver, Steven Osborne, Teresa Patterson and two pre-school children.

Oliver and Osborne were taken into custody on the below charges and transported to the Adams County Jail. The two children were taken into protective custody and released to the Children's Services Division. Teresa Patterson was taken into custody and transported to the Adams County Jail. Paul Patterson was contacted by Gold Mine Police Department and transported to his residence where he was placed in into custody and transported to the Adams County Jail.

Agents located several firearms including semi-automatic assault type weapons. Over 120 pounds of high grade marijuana was seized having a conservative street value estimation of $200,000.00 plus.

Seizures also included a large amount of construction tools, one jeep, $900.00, communications equipment, and the pole building and land with an estimated value of $65,000.00.........

SOUTH RIVER INTERAGENCY NARCOTICS TEAM
1975 MCPHERSON, ROOM 302
NORTH BEND, COLORADO 97444
(503) 942-7813

TO WHOM IT MAY CONCERN:

The following U.S. currency was seized by the South River Interagency Narcotics Team pursuant to Colorado Laws Chapter 791, Section 3(6):

DENOMINATION	AMOUNT
100's x 24	2,400
50's	
20's	
10's	
5's	
1's	

TOTAL $2,400.00

The above currency was verified by the following members of the South River Interagency Narcotics Team.

Laurie K. Kreutzer	R. Paul Fraiser
Name	Name
1975 McPherson Room #320	1975 McPherson Room #302
Address	Address
North Bend, Colorado 97459	North Bend, Colorado 97459
City, State, Zip PH#	City, State, Zip PH#
(503) 942-7813 ext. 559	(503) 942-7813 ext. 559

This money was turned over to authorities due to contamination.

This money is tainted with:
            [ ] Marijuana   [ ] Meth
            [ ] Cocaine   [ ] Other
            [ ] Heroin   **Unknown Narcotics**
            [X] Unknown

Signature _____   Date   10-08-94

Signature _____   Date   10-08-94

IN THE DISTRICT COURT OF THE STATE OF COLORADO
FOR ADAMS COUNTY

STATE OF COLORADO

      Plaintiff,

vs.   **SEARCH WARRANT**

Paul Patterson   Paul Jonah Patterson
                                 Paul S. Patterson
                                 Paul Jonah Paterson
                                 Paul Jonah Peterson
                                 Paul Jonah Pitterson
                                 Paul Jonah Putterson

IN THE NAME OF THE STATE OF COLORADO
TO ANY POLICE OFFICER IN THE STATE OF COLORADO, GREETINGS:

You are hereby commanded to search the:

XXX persons of   Paul Jonah Patterson DOB: 09-15-55

                        aka's

                        Paul S. Patterson
                        Paul Jonah Paterson
                        Paul Jonah Peterson
                        Paul Jonah Pitterson
                        Paul Jonah Putterson

XXX vehicles registered to or under the control of Paul Jonah Patterson and/or Teresa Patterson including but not limited to the following:

  1983 Jeep, Colorado license/LUVMUD
  1988 Dodge 4-door, Colorado license/RNN983
  1993 Terry RT, Colorado license/R667724

XXX premises located in the county of ADAMS described as follows: 2755 Shelly Road, Adams County, Colorado. To reach the property you would drive to Cripple Creek then drive west on 3rd Avenue from the Adams County Jail/Courthouse for approximately 1 and a half miles. As you reach the cross street of W. First Place, 3rd Avenue turns into Shelly Road. Approximately 1 mile from the Jail/Courthouse you will pass a Latter Day Saints Church, you will then continue on for about a half mile further when you will see a silver mailbox on the right side of the roadway. The numbers "2755" are on this mailbox. About 20 feet behind this mailbox is a wooden sign which reads "2755 Shelly Road" and has an arrow pointing up the left fork of the road. You would then drive up the roadway in the direction the arrow indicated. About 50 feet from the fork in the roadway you would see a green metal gate which has a sign which reads "Private property". The initial approximate 15 feet of the driveway leading to 2755 is concrete. The buildings on the property include a large, blue, metal shop/pole building with an opaque roof. There is a trailer on the property with a wooden shed attached to it. There is also a basement foundation that has been constructed for a residence. This is the Patterson residence as described above.

FOR: controlled substances including but not limited to processed marijuana; marijuana plants; marijuana seeds; equipment such as but not limited to high intensity light, halide lights and transformers, timers, irrigation equipment, fans, pumps, soil, pots, generators and other equipment used to manufacture marijuana; written records of equipment purchases and drug sales; evidence of domicile and control such as utility bills, telephone bills, credit cards, drivers licensed and business records; large sums of cash money from hundreds to thousands of dollars; evidence of the commercial nature of drug deals such as bank statements, tax records, cash money, safe deposit records and keys; weapons; equipment such as but not limited to scales, pruning shears and plastic baggies for packaging controlled substances; evidence of the conspiracy to manufacture, distribute and possess marijuana and to seize the aforesaid objects of the search; and

You are further directed to make return of this warrant to me within five (5) days after execution thereof.

( ) This warrant may be executed at any time of the day or night.

( ) This warrant may be executed more than five (5) but not more than ten (10) days from its date of issuance.

Issued over my hand on October 11, 1994 at 11:09 a.m.

| ADAMS COUNTY SHERIFF'S OFFICE |
NARCOTICS DETECTOR K-9 REPORT
1} CASE NO: 94-27813   CONNECT NO: SC94-202
2} DATE: 10/07/1994   3} TIME START: 0930   4} TIME END: 1140 5} TOTAL HOURS: 1
6} TYPE OF INCIDENT—TRAINING: SEARCH WARRANT   CALLOUT: X   OTHER: SUSPICIOUS CONDITIONS
7} TYPE OF ITEM SEARCHED—HOUSE: VEHICLE   STORAGE: OTHER: ARTICLE—CASH
8} LOCATION: STORAGE YARD, CRIPPLE CREEK BUILDING SUPPLY

9} TRAVEL TIME: 10   10} ON DUTY TIME: X   OFF DUTY TIME:
11} K-9 USED: PERCY   > ON LEAD: OFF LEAD: X

12} SEARCH WARRANT DATE: NA   13} AGENCY INVOLVED: NA
14} CASE OFFICER: NA   15} CASE FILE NUMBER: SC94-202
16} PERSONS ARRESTED/IF KNOWN— NAME   DOB   ADDRESS   CHARGE PATTERSON   09-15-55   2755 SHELY RD CRIPPLE CREEK OR NONE
17} NUMBER OF SEIZURES: 1   18} CURRENCY SEIZED: $ 2400.00
19} TESTED—YES: X   NO: PENDING: POSITIVE: X   NEGATIVE:
20} NARCOTICS SEIZED— TYPE   APPROX WEIGHT   APPROX VALUE NA
21} SCENE PHOTOGRAPHED—YES: NO: X SKETCHED—YES: NO: X
22} DESCRIBED ALERT: VERY STRONG BREATH CHG, AREA ALERT, WORK TO PINPT, GRAB ARTLS

23} TYPE OF DISTRACTIONS: BUILDING MATERIALS, PRODUCTS & VEHICLES
24} HANDLER/ID #> SGT. CRAIG ZANNI/505/08614/103   25} SHIFT: 02 26} DIST. 06

TRAINING
27} INDOOR SEARCH: OUTDOOR SEARCH: X COMPLETE WEATHER INFORMATION IF OUTDOOR SEARCH— WEATHER: FAIR TEMPERATURE: 65   WIND: 0   MPH   LIGHT:
28} TRAINING AIDS USED—COCAINE: NA   MARIJUANA   HEROIN: METHAMPHETAMINE: OTHER: DESCRIBE:
29} SAMPLE   AMOUNT BY WGT   PACKAGING   NA
30} AREA PRE SCENTED: YES   NO: X
31} SAMLE LOCATION(S) KNOWN TO HANDLER—YES: NO: X
32} STARTING POINT AND SEARCH PATTERN: SEE SYNOPSIS

SYNOPSIS—

On 10-07-94 I was contacted by a Curtis Jack, Manager for Cripple Creek Supply by phone. I was requested to respond to his location to do a check of a large amount of cash which he had received form a client with his business. Mr. Jack advised at that time he thought the presentation of a large amount of cash in large bills was suspicious and it also had an unusual odor about the money.

I subsequently responded to Cripple Creek Supply and made contact with Curtis Jack, Manager. At that time Mr. Jack indicated that a subject had come in the previous day to pay an account off with 24 one hundred dollar bills. Mr. Jack indicated that he felt the money very suspicious and had a strange odor about it.

I had Mr. Jack take the money and hide it in the lumberyard on the south end of the building. At that time Percy was allowed out of the kennel and we walked through the lumberyard area. As we neared a stack of lumber, Percy began to show a distinctive area alert and without command began crawling around the lumber and very distinctively and graphically alerted on the cash pointed out from a pile of lumber.

I advised Mr. Jack this was a positive reaction for a scent for which Percy was trained to detect. At that time he was issued a receipt and the $2400.00 dollars was seized for destruction as being contaminated cash. (See attached Interagency Narcotics Team Destruction Order.)

As a result I obtained additional information regarding the subject who brought in the cash identified as Teresa Patterson and her husband, Paul Jonah Patterson. It was found that the subject uses different spellings to his last name, including Peterson and Paterson and also Putterson. DOB 09-15-55, address: 2755 Shelly Road, Cripple Creek, OR. Colorado DL# 5353226. These items were obtained from a search of Sheriff's Office records.

At this time, the investigation is continuing. A check was obtained for the $2400.00 to repay Cripple Creek Supply as they are an innocent victim and that was turned over to Curtis Jack and the Cripple Creek Supply in Cripple Creek, OR, on the afternoon of 10-07-94.

CASE STATUS: Investigation is continuing.

ADAMS COUNTY SHERIFF'S OFFICE

INCIDENT NARRATIVE   /   FILE NO: 94-27813

DATE AND TIME TRANSCRIBED: Oct 19, 1994/ 11:29 am By: BJM

INCIDENT REPORT [ ]   RPT'D DATE/TIME [10-14-94]
SUPPLEMENTAL   [x]   OCC'D DATE/TIME [10-12-94]
CONNECT NUMBERS [SC94-206]

OFFENSE(S)   [Assist Police/Narcotics Investigation]
VICTIM'S NAME   [(S) Patterson, Paul]
LOCATION   [2755 Shelly Road, Cripple Creek, OR]

DISTRIBUTION   [SRINT 505]

SUMMARY:

On 10-12-94 I assisted members from SRINT and the Adams County Sheriff's Office in the service of a search warrant at 2755 Shelly Road, Cripple Creek, CO.

During the service of this search warrant an indoor marijuana growing operation was located at the pole building at that address and four people were arrested as a result.

PERSONS/INFORMATION:

(S) Patterson, Paul Jonah; DOB 09-15-55; 2755 Shelly Road, Cripple Creek, CO.

(S) Patterson, Teresa M; DOB 09-31-61; 2755 Shelly Road, Cripple Creek, CO.

(S) Oliver, Peter; W/M/A; NFI

(AO) Detective Sgt. Zanni, Craig; Adams County Sheriff's Office.

(AO) Detective Looney, Dan; Adams County Sheriff's Office, currently assigned to SRINT.

(AO) Sgt. Moorman, Jim; Adams County Sheriff's Office.

ADAMS COUNTY SHERIFF'S OFFICE

INCIDENT NARRATIVE   /   FILE NO: 94-27813

DATE AND TIME TRANSCRIBED: Oct 19, 1994/ 11:29 am By: BJM

(AO) Detective Ranger, Vince; Colorado State Police, Adams,, currently assigned to SRINT.

(AO) Officer Foster, Paul; Adams Police Department, currently assigned to SRINT.

(AO) Sgt. Benz, Tom; Colorado State Police, Adams, currently assigned to SRINT as Coordinator.

EVIDENCE/PROPERTY INFORMATION:

(E) One Adams County Sheriff's Office Inventory Seizure Form listing items seized by myself during the service of the search warrant. All items marked with my initials and listed on the inventory form as JPD—001 through JPD—027.

All items seized by myself and marked with my initials were from the ground floor of the shop at 2755 Shelly Road, Cripple Creek.

Evidence submitted to Evidence Custodian at the scene.

VEHICLE INFORMATION:

(SV) One white, 70's model, Chevy Nova with California License: 552RGQ

Reportedly owned by Peter Oliver.
OBSERVATIONS:

On 10-12-94 at approximately 0830 hours I met with officers from the South River Interagency Narcotics Team (SRINT) in the Adams County Sheriff's Office for a briefing regarding a search warrant to be served at 2755 Shelly Road, Cripple Creek, OR. During the briefing I was assigned as a searcher and was requested to remain with other officers at the Sheriff's Office until requested by Sgt. Zanni.

After the briefing was concluded, an initial contingence of officers left the Sherif's Office in route to 2755 Shelly Road and at approximately 0900 hours I was requested to respond with other officers to that location. At approximately 0905 hours I arrived at the address of Shelly Road and a white Chevy Nova was parked on the property, upon my arrival I was contacted by Sgt. Moorman who requested I search for California license 552RGQ. Sgt. Moorman advised me that he had received consent from the reported owner, Peter Oliver, who was currently being interviewed by Detective Sgt. Zanni. In searching that vehicle I seized miscellaneous paperwork and address books that were located in the glove compartment of that vehicle that bore the name of Peter Oliver.

After I concluded searching the Chevy Nova, I was then assigned to assist searching the ground floor of the green metal pole building on the property.

In searching the ground floor portion of the metal pole building, I seized items marked JPD—002 through JPD—027. Items marked JPD—006, JPD—007, and JPD—008 are three rifles that were located in the ground floor area, an AR-15, a Mossberg bolt action rifle I located on a couch on the ground floor, after these weapons had been secured by initial responding officers. I located and seized a Marlin, lever action rifle that was the afternoon hours driving a white Chevy Nova which was currently present of the property. He stated that he was visiting and was in the green building upon our arrival; however, he did not know anything about any marijuana being grown at that location.

Mr. Oliver stated that he was a surfer and knew nothing about the marijuana grow or the processing of marijuana at that location. He indicated that the previous evening and morning he had some marijuana with Steven Osborn who was present but he did not know where the marijuana had come from and Steven had the bud when they started smoking.

Mr. Oliver indicated that his property was in the building and he was present when ____ and he had spent the evening before the night of 10-11-94, sleeping in the shop on a mattress at that location. Mr. Oliver indicated that he had no knowledge of the activities on the property or anything regarding the marijuana or what was occurring at that location.

Clearance Codes: Cleared by arrest.

ACTION(S) PENDING:

Refer to the South River Interagency Narcotics Team for prosecution.

ADAMS COUNTY SHERIFF'S OFFICE
NARCOTICS DETECTOR K-9 REPORT
1} CASE NO: 94-27813   CONNECT NO: SC94-206
2} DATE: 10/12/94 TIME START: 0830 4} TIME END: 1230 5} TOTAL HOURS: 4
6} TYPE OF INCIDENT—TRAINING: SEARCH WARRANT: X   CALLOUT: OTHER:
7} TYPE OF ITEM SEARCHED—HOUSE: X VEHICLE: STORAGE: OTHER: STORAGE SHED AND PROPERTY
8} 2755 SHELLY ROAD, CRIPPLE CREEK, OR
9} TRAVEL TIME: 10   10} ON DUTY TIME: X   OFF DUTY TIME:
11} K-9 USED: Percy   > ON LEAD: OFF LEAD: X
12} SEARCH WARRANT DATE: 10/11/94 13} AGENCY INVOLED: SCINT
14} CASE OFFICER: PAUL FOSTER 15]} CASE FILE NUMBER: SC94-206
16} PERSONS ARRESTED/IF KNOWN
NAME   DOB   ADDRESS   CHARGES
PATTERSON, PAUL   091555   2755 SHELLY RD, CRIPPLE CREEK   PCS

PATTERSON, TERESA	093161	2755 SHELLY RD, CRIPPLE CREEK	PCS
OLIVER, PETER A.	022960	OXNARD, CA	PCS
OSBORNE, STEVEN E.	020757	MONTEREY, CA	PCS

17} NUMBER OF SEIZURES: 18} CURRENCY SEIZED: $900.00

19} TESTED—YES: NO: PENDING: X
              POSITIVE: NEGATIVE:

20} NARCOTICS SEIZED

TYPE	APPROX WEIGHT	APPROX VALUE
MARIJUANA	59,989 GRAMS	$500,000.00

21} SCENE PHOTOGRAPHED—YES: X   NO:
              SKETCHED—YES: NO: X

22}DESCRIBED ALERT: VERY GRAPHIC, DISTINCTIVE

23} TYPE OF DISTRACTIONS: NUMEROUS PERSONS, BUILDING
MATERIALS

24} HANDLER/ID #> SGT. CRAIG ZANNI/505/08614/103 SHIFT: 02
26} DIST: 06

DATE/TIME TRANSCRIBED:	BY: DLL

SUPPLEMENTAL [X]   CONTINUATION [ ]   CONNECT NO. [SC94-206]

OCC'D DATE/TIME [10-12-94/0855 hrs.   ]
VICTIM'S NAME   [State of Colorado   ]
OFFENSE   [MCS, CMCS, CPCS, PCS—Marij., Child Neg.   ]

DISTRIBUTION TO   [SRINT—DA   ]

EVIDENCE/PROPERTY:

E-1) DLL—001—Ohaus weigh scales, scissors w/ marij. Residue, and roach clip forceps w/ marij. Residue.

Located in the pole building upstairs on the coffee table.

Placed into evidence at the ACSO/SRINT.

E-2) DLL—002—"Makita" drill, 2 batteries and a charger.

Located in the pole building upstairs on the coffee table.

Placed into evidence at ACSO/SRINT

E-3) DLL—003—Marijuana (face) pipe w/ residue, film canister w/ marijuana & S.J.K (?) written on top, (2) two drinking glasses (for latent prints).

Located in the pole building upstairs on the coffee table.

Placed into evidence at the ACSO/SRINT.

E-4) DLL—004—Box w/ "glad" zip lock bags (to package the marijuana).

Located in the pole building upstairs on the coffee table.

Placed into evidence at the ACSO/SRINT.

E-5) DLL—005—"Reddy Heater" kerosene heater.
Located in the upstairs of the pole building (it was working when we arrived).
Placed into evidence at the ACSO/SRINT.

DATE/TIME TRANSCRIBED: **BY: DLL**

E-6) DLL—006—"Vornado" Table fan

Located in the upstairs of the pole building (it was working when we arrived).

Placed into evidence at the ACSO/SRINT.

E-7) DLL—007—"Sony" AM-FM Cassette Player, orange extension cord, and a power strip w/ Patterson's name printed upon it.

Located in the pole building upstairs.

Placed into evidence at the ACSO/SRINT.

E-8) DLL—008—"Dynasty" Floor stand fan.

Located in the pole building upstairs.

Placed into evidence at the ACSO/SRINT.

E-9) DLL—009—a Brown Paper Bag (BPB) containing Marijuana bud.

Located in the pole building upstairs.

Placed into evidence at the ACSO/SRINT.

E-10) DLL—010—BPB w/ shoe box cont. marijuana, (2) two scissors w/ marijuana residue, and a bottle of rubbing alcohol.

Located in the pole building upstairs on a wooden T.V. tray.

Placed into evidence at the ACSO/SRINT.

E-11) DLL—011—(1) one paper bag containing processed marijuana bud and a zip lock bag of weighed marijuana.

Located in the pole building upstairs.

Placed into evidence at the ACSO/SRINT.

E-12) DLL—012—"Pro-Gro" climate control GC-19

Located in the pole building upstairs.

DATE/TIME TRANSCRIBED: **BY: DLL**

Placed into evidence at the ACSO/SRINT.

E-13) DLL—013—(1) empty Coors can, (2) Coke cans.

Located in the pole building upstairs.

Placed into evidence at the ACSO/SRINT.

E-14) DLL—014—(1) Metal can w/ marijuana roach cig. Butts (can have latent prints on the outside.

Located in the pole building upstairs near the coffee table.

Placed into evidence at the ACSO/SRINT.

E-15) DLL—015—(2) Brn Paper Bags w/ marijuana bud and leaves.

Located in the pole building upstairs.

Placed into evidence at the ACSO/SRINT.

E-16) DLL—016—Shop Vacuum with attachments.

Located in the pole building upstairs.

Placed into evidence at the ACSO/SRINT.

E-17) DLL—017—"Troy-Built" Rototiller-chipper Mdl.# 12058, SN# 120580306332.

Located across the driveway from the shop (under a tarp).

Placed into evidence at the ACSO/SRINT.

E-18) DLL—018—Orange extension ladder.

Located hanging on a rack attached to the back of the pole building.

Placed into evidence at the ACSO/SRINT.

E-19) DLL—019—Stihl 036 chainsaw w/ 28" bar, SN# 225036971

Located on the bottom floor of the pole building next to the front door.

DATE/TIME TRANSCRIBED: **BY: DLL**

Placed into evidence at the ACSO/SRINT.

E-20) DLL—020—Evidence of domicile for Thomas Osborn.

Located on the bottom floor of the pole building in a suitcase. Located by Sgt. Benz.

Placed into evidence at the ACSO/SRINT.

E-21) DLL—021—(1) one US M8A1 bayonet with sheath.

Located on the top shelf of the porch which is attached to the camp trailer.

Placed into evidence at the ACSO/SRINT.

SUMMARY:

On 10-12-94 at approximately 0855 hrs. I assisted SRINT and other Police Officers execute a search warrant at 2755 Shelly Rd., Cripple Creek, CO. Paul Patterson, Teresa Patterson, Steven Osborn, and Peter Oliver were arrested on various drug and child endangering/neglect charges.

ADD'L PERSONS/INFORMATION:

S-1) Patterson, Paul Jonah. 09-15-55, WMA, 600/180, BRO/BLU, Address: 2755 Shelly Road, Cripple Creek, CO. Phone # (503) 396-6007.

S-2) Patterson, Teresa Matthews. 09-31-61, WFA, 508/170, BRO/BRO,. Address: 2755 Shelly Road, Cripple Creek, CO. Phone # (503) 396-6007.

S-3) Osborn, Steven Edward. 02-07-57, WMA, 601/200, BRO/BRO, CDL# N3138444. Address: 440 David St., Monterey, CA 93940.

S-4) Oliver, Peter A. 02-29-60, WMA, 603/185, BLN/HZL, CDL# N6282424. Address: 5033 Terramar Way, Oxnard, CA 93035. Phone # (806) 985-4345.

DATE/TIME TRANSCRIBED:	BY: DLL

W) Det. Vince Ranger, OSP/SRINT, 756-2020 x516

W) Det. Sgt. Craig Zanni, ACSO, 756-2020 x378

W) Det. Pat Downing, ACSO, 756-2020 x381

W) Det. Mike Brinkley, ACSO/SRINT, 756-2020 x516

W) Sgt. Jim Moorman, ACSO, 756-2020 x374

W) Trooper Ashenfelter, OSP, 269-5999

W) Sgt. Tom Benz, OSP/SRINT, 756-2020 x577

W) Sgt. Ron Wampole, BPD/SRINT, 347-2241

OBSERVATIONS:

On 10-12-94 at approximately 0855 hrs. I assisted SRINT and other officers with the execution of a search warrant at 2755 Shelly Road, Cripple Creek, OR.

After securing the scene we learned there had been two men in the pole building when we arrived. These men were identified as Osborn, Steven and Oliver, Peter. Det. Ranger, Det. Foster and I located Teresa Patterson and two of her young children in the camp trailer.

We advised Mrs. Patterson we were there because of complaints that she and her husband were growing marijuana in the pole building. We asked her for permission to search the pole building. Mrs. Patterson said yes then seemed to catch herself and she quickly asked if we had a "search warrant". Det. Ranger advised her yes we did has a search warrant. Trooper Ashenfelter read the search warrant and the Miranda warnings to Mrs. Patterson.

We were advised by other officers that they had discovered the entire top floor of the pole building contained drying/harvested marijuana.

Det. Ranger and I interview Mrs. Patterson about the marijuana grow. See the statements section and Det. Ranger's report for more detail. I was assigned to take 35mm photographs of the scene and the evidence located by the searching officers. Det. Ranger and I also video tape recorded the scene.

DATE/TIME TRANSCRIBED: **BY: DLL**

As we entered the pole building we immediately smelled the strong, overwhelming odor of green marijuana. While walking through the lower floor of the pole building we noticed there were flakes of marijuana littering the tops of the belongings stored there (the lower floor was filled with household belongings). At the far end of the path through the belongings, I observed a long work bench & tool racks. This work bench was within a few feet of the hole in the veiling which allowed access to the upstairs grow/drying room. Resting upon the work bench was an electronic baby monitoring intercom. Beside the work bench I observed a small baby crib, which contained baby toys and small fragments of marijuana.

I climbed up the ladder (which I found under the access hole) and into the marijuana grow/drying room. I found myself standing in front a large wooden coffee table. On the coffee table I observed the following: marijuana residue; a triple beam "Ohaus" scales (with marijuana residue); scissors with marijuana residue; freezer bags; half eaten food & chips; and other items of evidence. See the photos for more detail. Under the coffee table we found the box for the weigh scales, an open box of freezer bags, and marijuana residue. Beside the coffee table I noticed chairs, a wooden T.V. tray (which had a cardboard box containing marijuana which was being processed), a brown paper bag which contained a processed marijuana bud and freezer bag of weighed marijuana.

Next we observed rows of hanging marijuana. The marijuana limbs were handing upside down from the lines which spanned the grow room. In the middle of the room, nailed to the ceiling, we observed a heavy duty netting had been nailed to the rafters. Using a step ladder we looked onto the netting and found that half of it was covered drying harvested marijuana bud.

As we looked around the room we found a Kerosene/electric heater was running pushing warm air into the marijuana drying room). There were several fans which were running and we plugged into a power-strip. The power-strip had the name "PATTERSON" hand printed upon it. We found a "Pro-Gro" GC-19 climate control panel screwed to the wall. There were two cords next to the box. These two cords led to the two large wall mounted exhaust fans. The fan on the back side of the pole building was running when we arrived. The floor of the marijuana grow/drying room was painted white as were some of the rafters. This is a common practice of marijuana growers (for the reflecting of light). There were round, dirty, evenly spaced grow.

pot circles visible on the floor throughout the grow room. We also noticed that black plastic had been stapled to the upper rafters of the grow room. (NOTE: It was obvious from the semi-clear corrugated roofing which had been used in the construction of the room that the marijuana plants had been grown "greenhouse style".) One interesting aspect of the marijuana grow room was the empty boxes, pieces of boxed, and clothing which had been stapled or placed next to the walls of the grow room (driveway side). These items had been placed there as window dressing so that when a person in the driveway looked up at the upper story of building, it looked as if it were being used as storage.

After we completed our initial survey Sgt. Wampole arrived with Paul Patterson. Det. Ranger and I interviewed Patterson. See the statements section for more detail.

While walking around the property we located 45 marijuana stalk root balls hidden behind a mound of dirt. The root balls had been turned over so the marijuana stalk stumps were not visible to visitors. The root balls had been taken out of the large planter pots which they had been grown in. The used planter pots were located on the back side of the pole building. We also found a new (plastic wrapped) bundle of planter pots near the used ones.

Det. Foster located (4) four potted rotting male marijuana plants which had been discarded beside a trail behind the camp trailer. Det. Ranger, Sgt. Wampole and I collected evidence form the upper story (grow/harvest room) of the pole building.

On 10-13-94 Det. Foster and I served Mr. Osborn, Mr. Oliver, Mr. Patterson, and Mrs. Patterson with forfeiture papers. While we were in the jail waiting for Mr. Osborn, I talked with Deputy Donna Westover. Deputy Westover advised me Osborn told her that he and his friend had just come up to see his friend's marijuana grow.

On 10-15-94 I spoke to Benny Thurman who told me that Mr. and Mrs. Patterson still owe him $1786.00 for the construction of the pole building. The total cost of the pole building was over $8,000.00. Mr. Thurman told me he did not build a second floor in the pole building.

STATEMENTS:
Teresa Patterson stated in substance that she did not know anything

DATE/TIME TRANSCRIBED: **BY: DLL**

about a marijuana grow in the pole building. She just thought her husband was building "something" up there. She said she does the laundry, takes showers and spends time in the lower floor of the pole building. She advised us her children play Nintendo in the pole building. Mrs. Patterson said she has not smelled any marijuana in or around the building. Later Mrs. Patterson admitted she did know her husband was growing "a couple" of marijuana plants upstairs in the pole building. She admitted she had smelled the marijuana which her husband was growing. Mrs. Patterson also told us her husband uses marijuana for his bad back although she admitted he does not have a prescription for the marijuana. Mrs. Patterson said she and her husband had been arrested in 1983 for marijuana related charges. Her husband spent time in jail and she was placed on diversion. After her diversion she had her record cleared.

Mrs. Patterson told us the property was paid for and they used her husband's settlement check to pay for the property. She said he received a $28,000.00 check (after other fees) from California Casualty for a back injury he received as a carpenter in California.

We asked Mrs. Patterson about the numerous firearms, which were lying about the residence and the pole building, and she told us the pistols belonged to her while the rifles and shotguns belonged to her husband.

Paul Patterson stated in substance that the marijuana grow was his but he admitted his wife knew the marijuana grow was there. Mr. Patterson said he had grown about 25 plants, each plant being 8 feet tall and very bushy (indicating a wide circle with his arms). Mr. Patterson told us he had started growing the marijuana plants in March of 1994. He said that was his first grow in ten years and he was only growing it for personal use. He said he was not growing for the money and he might not have grown again for 8-9 years. (NOTE: We pointed out to Mr. Patterson that it is common knowledge in the marijuana community that marijuana THC levels drop rapidly over time. This makes storage of a large amount of marijuana "for personal use" a convenient excuse but not realistic.)

Mr. Patterson went on to say he has been known to give marijuana away to his friends. We asked Patterson why he was growing marijuana when he had a good job. He answered that friends talked him into it and the money...He went on to gripe that he shouldn't have let his friends talk him into growing the marijuana. But Mr. Patterson would not give us the names of the "friends" who had helped him set up the grow.

DATE/TIME TRANSCRIBED: **BY: DLL**

He insisted the marijuana was for "personal use" and it was not for sale because the last time he got into more trouble because the marijuana was for sale.

Mr. Patterson described the marijuana grow as follows: He said he started the plants from seeds and planted them in dirt although he said he had been setting up the grow room for a hydroponic grow. He commented that we must have seen the PVC piping which was lying on the floor of the grow. When asked, he told us he had thrown out (4) four male marijuana plants (he pointed towards the trail where the male plants had been found). Also when asked, he told us the black plastic sheeting (stapled above the drying plants) had been placed there so the drying marijuana would not sour. "Because the smoke gets sour if they dry in the sun." Patterson said the planter pots behind the pole building were the ones he had used to grow his marijuana plants in.

Mr. Patterson told us Peter had just arrived and Steven is a friend from Monterey, California. Steven had told him he could get someone to help harvest the marijuana grow and on the next day Peter had arrived. Patterson said Steven and Peter were staying in the area we were in (indicating the lower floor of the pole building). Patterson told us they were there to help "break down the grow".

Patterson said he and his wife had lived in Cripple Creek for approximately 3 years. Their previous address was 1025 N. Dean, Cripple Creek, OR, he said. They moved up onto the property at 2755 Shelly Road about one year ago. They purchased their camp trailer from on time from GIB'S in Adams,. They purchased the property for $49,000.00 and had Benny Thurman build the pole building on the property. He said he used the last bit of the settlement money to pay the property off. Patterson said he still owes about $2,000.00 to Thurman for the pole building. The pole building was built in December 1993. When the building was built it did not have a second floor. Patterson admitted that he had added the second floor on to the pole building.

Patterson told us he had gotten a $42,500.00 settlement check from a combination of insurance companies in California for injuries he had received there.

In answer to a question about the firearms, Patterson told us the rifles belong to him and the pistols belong to his wife. Then in the next breath, Patterson said his wife gave the one .357 pistol to him as an anniversary present two years ago. Patterson indicated he could not own a pistol because he is a felon but in California he can own a rifle.

TRAINING
27} INDOOR SEARCH: OUTDOOR SEARCH: X COMPLETE WEATHER INFORMATION IF OUTDOOR SEARCH— WEATHER: OVERCAST TEMPERATURE: 65   WIND: 0   MPH   LIGHT: DAY
28} TRAINING AIDS USED—COCAINE: NA   MARIJUANA: HEROIN: METHAMPHETAMINE: OTHER: DESCRIBE:
29} SAMPLE   AMOUNT BY WEIGHT (GRAMS)   PACKAGING   NA
30} AREA PRE SCENTED—YES: X   NO:
31} SAMPLE LOCATION(S) KNOWN TO HANDLER—YES: NA   NO:
32} STARTING POINT AND SEARCH PATTERN: STANDARD SEARCH PATTERNS

FOR THE COUNTY OF ADAMS

THE STATE OF COLORADO
          PLAINTIFF
    VS.
PAUL JONAH PATTERSON

RECORD OF PROCEEDINGS
AND ORDER

Case No. <u>94CR1763</u>

The following proceedings were held in the above-captioned case before the undersigned judge on <u>10-13-94.</u>

_____ District Attorney appearing for the State.

(X) Arraignment/New Charge/Continued/DA Info/Detainer/Fugitive Complaint
( ) Arraignment-Probation Violation/Contempt/RO Violation/Diversion Violation
( ) Defendant failed to appear. B/W ordered, Security/Bail set $_____.
( ) Other _____

( ) Defendant appeared with counsel _____
(X) Defendant appeared without counsel, was informed of right to retained or appointed counsel and the court appointed <u>not eligible for court-appointed counsel</u>/continued proceedings to _____ so defendant could retain counsel.
( ) Defendant waived rights to counsel.

(X) Defendant advised of right to jury trial/hearing and confrontation, privilege against self-incrimination, and all other procedures and penalties required by law.

( ) Counsel for defendant waived reading of accusatory instrument, acknowledged receipt of a certified true copy.
(X) The Court ( ) district attorney, read the indictment/information/ fugitive complaint to the defendant/delivered a certified true copy to the defendant.

( ) Defendant waived Identity Hearing/Writ of Habeas Corpus/Extradition and signed a waiver and the court ordered defendant be held _____ days.

( ) Defendant ordered to report to jail forthwith to be booked and released.
( ) Defendant entered a plea of ( ) Not Guilty ( ) Guilty ( ) Divert ( ) No Contest ( ) Admitted Probation Violation to the following charges:

_____

( ) Other: _____
( ) Pay $ _____ By _____ and balance at $_____ Month beginning _____ Or appear at 9AM next Judicial Day.

(X) THE ABOVE CASE HAS BEEN GIVEN A DAY AND TIME CERTIFICATION FOR:
    PV/Omni/Identity/Preliminary/Extradition/RO <u>10-19-94</u> at <u>8:30 AM</u>
    Writ of Habeas Corpus/Contempt of Court: _____ at _____
    Plea: _____ at _____. Sentencing: _____ at _____
    Trial: _____ at _____
    PSI: ( ) Requested ( ) Waived ( ) Further Time Waved

Other: _____
( ) Cancel date of: _____.
( ) _____ Dismissed Pursuant to Plea bargain.

The following arrangements were made for the release of the defendant:
( ) Release on own recognizance   ( ) Security set at $ 250,000.00
( ) Defendant held in custody   ( ) Bail set at $ _____

Dated 10-13-94   Reporter Betsy Barrett   _____
                                          District/Circuit Judge

F-94-2620-1/CN

IN THE CIRCUIT COURT OF THE STATE OF COLORADO
FOR ADAMS COUNTY

THE STATE OF COLORADO   INDICTMENT
       PLAINTIFF,
      VS.   Case No. 94CR1763
PAUL JONAH PATTERSON
       DEFENDANT.
   DOB: 09-15-55

Paul Jonah Patterson is accused by the Grand Jury for the County of
Adams, State or Colorado, by this Indictment of the crime(s) of

COUNT 1: CONSPIRACY TO MANUFACTURE/DELIVER
CONTROLLED SUBSTANCE, COS 161.450/475.992, Class AF

COUNT 2: MANUFACTURE/DELIVER CONTROLLED SUSBSTANCE,
COS 475.992, Class AF

COUNT 3: CONSPIRACY TO DELIVER CONTROLLED SUBSTANCE
FOR CONSDERATION, COS 161.450/475.992, Class BF

COUNT 4: DELIVER CONTROLLED SUBSTANCE FOR
CONSIDERATION, COS 475.992, Class BF

COUNT 5: CONSPIRACY TO POSSESS CONTROLLED SUBSTANCE,
COS 161.450/475.992, Class BF

COUNT 6: POSSESSION OF CONTROLLED SUBSTANCE, COS
475.992, Class BF

COUNT 7, 8 & 9: CHILD NEGLECT IN THE FIRST DEGREE, COS
163.547, Class BF

COUNT 10, 11 & 12: ENDANGERING THE WELFARE OF A MINOR,
COS 163.575, Class AM

COUNT 13-24: FELON IN POSSESSION OF A FIREARM, COS
166.270, CLASS CF

COMMITTED AS FOLLOWS:
COUNT 1:
The said defendant, between the 1st day of January, 1994 and
the 12th day of October, 1994, in Adams County, Colorado, did
unlawfully, with the intent that conduct constituting the crime of
manufacture of a controlled substance, punishable as a felony be
performed, agree with Teresa Patterson, and a person or persons
unknown to engage in the performance of the following conduct: to

unlawfully and knowingly manufacture marijuana, a schedule I controlled substance; The State further alleges that the above-described manufacture involved substantial quantities, to-wit: 150 or more grams of marijuana substance;

The State further alleges that the above-described manufacture was a commercial drug offense accompanied by the following: 1) The defendant was in possession of firearms for the purpose of using them in connection with this controlled substance offense; 2) The defendant was in possession of materials being used for the packaging of controlled substances, other than the material being used to contain the substance that was the subject of this offense; 3) This offense involved modifications of a structure by painting, wiring, plumbing or lighting to facilitate a controlled substance offense; 4) The defendant was in possession of manufacturing paraphernalia, including recipes, precursor chemicals, laboratory equipment, ventilating or power generating equipment; 5) The defendant was in possession of great than 110 grams of marijuana substance; and 6) The defendant was, at the time of the crimes, unlawfully in possession of firearms.

COUNT 2:
The said defendant, between the 1st day of January, 1994 and the 12th day of October, 1994, in Adams County, Colorado, did unlawfully, and knowingly manufacture marijuana, a schedule I controlled substance;

The State further alleges that the above-described manufacture involved substantial quantities, to-wit: 150 or more grams of marijuana substance;

The State further alleges that the above-described manufacture was a commercial drug offense accompanied by the following: 1) The defendant was in possession of firearms for the purpose of using them in connection with this controlled substance offense; 2) The defendant was in possession of materials being used for the packaging of controlled substances, other than the material being used to contain the substance that was the subject of this offense; 3) This offense involved modifications of a structure by painting, wiring, plumbing or lighting to facilitate a controlled substance offense; 4) The defendant was in possession of manufacturing paraphernalia, including recipes, precursor chemicals, laboratory equipment, ventilating or power generating equipment; 5) The defendant was in possession of great than 110 grams of marijuana substance; and 6) The defendant was, at the time of the crimes, unlawfully in possession of firearms.

COUNT 13:
The said defendant, between the 1st day of January, 1994 and the 12th day of October, 1994, in Adams County, Colorado, having

previously been convicted in this state or any other state of the United States, of a felony, did unlawfully and knowingly possess a firearm, to-wit: a Ruger 10-22 rifle.

IN THE DISTRICT COURT OF THE STATE OF COLORADO
FOR ADAMS COUNTY

STATE OF COLORADO
       PLAINTIFF   **RETURN OF SEARCH WARRANT**
       VS.
PAUL JONAH PATTERSON
AKA'S
MARK S. PATTERSON
PAUL JONAH PATERSON
PAUL JONAH PETERSON
PAUL JONAH PITTERSON
PAUL JONAH PUTTERSON

ET. AL.

      DEFENDANTS

STATE OF COLORADO   )
) **ss**
COUNTY OF ADAMS   )

      I, the undersigned police officer, executed the attached warrant on October12, 1994, at 9:00 a.m., and state that the following is a true list of things seized by me pursuant to warrant. See the attached list.

_____
               Signature of Officer Detective

Subscribed and sworn to before me this 17th day of October, 1994.

_____
                       Judge

SC94-206   [X] Adams Co.   [ ] Gold Mine PD   [ ] Myrtle Point PD
             [ ] Cripple Creek PD [ ] O.S.P.   [ ] Adams, PD

INCIDENT NO. 94-27813
  E: 10/12/94 TIME: 0855

DEFENDANT: PATTERSON, PAUL AND TERESA

ITEMS TAKEN PURSUANT TO A SEARCH (CONSENT/WARRANT) OF:
2755 Shelly Rd.; 1983 Jeep OR LIC LUVMUD; 1988 Dodge 4-door OR
LIC RNN983; 1993 Terry RT OR LIC R667724

RECORDING OFFICER: W. Little   PHOTOGRAPHS BY: D. Looney/Shills

OFFICERS ASSISTING: Ranger, Foster, Zanni, Benz, Wampole,
Moorman, Ashenfenter, Brinkley

Officer	Items seized	Location found
JPD-002-005	(19) Baggies of Marij bud	Rafters ground floor of shop
JPD-001	Bag w/ misc paper work & address book	White nova CA Lic. 552RGQ
JPD-006	AR 15A2 w/ blk carrying case & 3 clips	Ground floor shop
JPD-007	Mosberg Rifle bolt action	Ground floor shop
JPD-008	Marlin Rifle Lever action	Ground floor shop
JPD-009	Belt w/ ammo & holster	Hanging by work bench (shop)
VAR-001	(2) Boxes marij shake, loose marij stocks	Upstairs of shop—coffee table
DLL-001	Ohaus scales, scissors w/ marij residue	Upstairs of shop—coffee table
	Roach clip, forceps w/ marij residue	Upstairs of shop—coffee table
DLL-002	1 "Mahita" drill, 2 batteries & charger	Upstairs of shop—coffee table
JPD-010	Wooden ammo box w/ shotgun ammo	Ground floor—shop
JPD-011	Metal ammo box w/ empty clips	Ground floor—shop
JPD-012	Metal ammo box w/ ammo	Ground floor—shop
JPD-013	Cookie tin w/ loose marij	Table saw—ground floor (shop)
VAR-002	Plastic bag w/ (22) bundles of marij	Upstairs (shop)
VAR-003	Plastic bag w/ (24) bundles of marij	Upstairs shop

DLL-003	Marij pipe w/residue, film canister w/ marij & S.J.K written on top, (2) drinking glasses to be printed	Upstairs (shop)
DLL-004	Box w/ "Glad" zip lock bags	Upstairs (shop)
VAR-004	Plastic bag w/ (25) bundles of marij	Upstairs (shop)
DLL-005	"Reddy Heater" Kerosene heater	Upstairs (shop)
DLL-006	"Vornado" table fan	Upstairs (shop)
DLL-007	"Sony" Cassette player, Extension cord & power strip w/ Patterson's name on it	
DLL-008	"Dynasty" floor stand	Upstairs (shop)
VAR-005	Plastic bag w/ (31) bundles marij	Upstairs (shop)
DLL-009	BPB w/ marij bud	Upstairs (shop)
VAR-006	Plastic bag w/ (2) bundles marij	Upstairs (shop)
VAR-007	Plastic bag w/ (33) bundles marij	Upstairs (shop)
VAR-008	Plastic bag w/ (25) bundles marij	Upstairs (shop)
DLL-010	BPB w/ shoe box marij, (2) Scissors & rubbing alcohol	Upstairs (shop)
DLL-011	Bag processed marij w/ zip lock bag of weighed marij	Upstairs (shop)
JPD-014	Loose marij	Downstairs (shop)
JPD-015	Loose marij in plastic container	Downstairs (shop)
JPD-016	Misc ammo in cardboard box & containers	
JPD-017	Fire-crackers	Downstairs (shop)
JPD-018	"Foodsaver" vacuum packing system	Downstairs (shop)
DLL-012	"Pro-Gro" climate control GC-19	Upstairs (shop)
VAR-009	BPB w/ marij stems	Upstairs (shop)
JPD-019	Day pack sack w/ "Canon" camera	Downstairs (shop)
JPD-020	Tray w/ loose marij	Downstairs (shop)
JPD-021	Dry marij in white B-Mart sack	Downstairs (shop)
JPD-022	Kerosene & electric heater w/ blower	Downstairs (shop)
VAR-010	Lrg. Plastic container w/ misc grow equip	Upstairs (shop)

VAR-011	Numerous plastic plant ID Tags	Upstairs (shop)
DLL-013	1 Coors & 2 Coke cans- empty	Upstairs (shop)
DLL-014	1 metal can w/ marij roaches	Upstairs (shop)
DLL-015	2 BPB w/ marij bud & leaves	Upstairs (shop)
DLL-016	Shop vacuum	Downstairs (shop)
VAR-012	3 Oackra plants	Upstairs (shop)
JPD-023	Loose marij in 2 cans	Above TV downstairs
RGW-001	Starter light 70 wt with Peat Moss	Ceiling rafter above work bench in shop
VAR-013	"Camel" tin w/ 1 cig, pair of forceps w/ marij residue	In Jeep lic. LUVMUD
DLL-017	"Troy-Built" rototiller-chipper Mod 12058 SN # 120580306332	In yard by clothesline
VAR-014	Jeep OR Lic. LUVMUD 1983 Mod Blu and primer	Parked at residence
IPD-024	Plastic container w/ financial Records and photos	File cabinet downstairs (shop)
DLL-018	Org extension ladder	Behind shop
VAR-015	Marij ID tags, sample pot & stalk out of (49)	Over bank by shop
VAR-016	Stihl 009L Chainsaw SN # 227320224	Downstairs (shop)
VAR-017	Mod 77 SN HB404309	Downstairs (shop)
DLL-019	Stihl 036 chainsaw w/ 28" bar SN 225036971	Downstairs (shop)
DLL-020	Evid of domicile for *	Suitcase downstairs
JPD-025	Wooden box w/ misc ammo	Under work bench downstairs
VAR-018	1 Sentry safe Red	Downstairs (shop)
JPD-026	"Radio Shack" handheld CB	Downstairs (shop)
TB-001	Box of Records	Downstairs (shop)
JPD-027	2 org heavy duty ext. cords	Downstairs (shop)
TB-002	Table saw "Delta" 10" SN 93096203 Base SN 92E96921	Downstairs (shop)

SRINT

Incident No. <u>SC94-206</u>   Date: <u>10-12-94</u>   Time: <u>8:55 A</u>

Defendant: <u>Patterson, Paul and Teresa</u>

Items taken pursuant to a search warrant of: <u>2755 Shelly Rd; 1983 Jeep OR Lic. LUVMUD; 1988 Dodge 4-door OR Lic. RNN983; 1993 Terry RT OR Lic. R667724</u>

Recording Officer: <u>Ashenfelter</u>   Photographs by: <u>Looney</u>

Officers assisting: Ranger, Foster, Looney, Zanni, Wampole, Moorman, Brinkley, Benz, Whittle

Officer	Item seized	Location found
MMB001	$900 currency in white envelope	Lock box under bed in front bedroom
MMB002	Sentry lock box w/ misc documents	Under bed in front bedroom
PLF001	Ruger 10/22 ser# 23637584 Stainless steel rifle	Above front door
MMB003	Plastic airline box Containing Ruger 22 Pistol mark II Ser# 215-58839	Under bed in front bedroom
MMB004	Brown camera box containing 2 Cameras. 1. Canon EOI 35mm 2833588 w/ film 2. Canon AE-1 35mm 5089024 misc. accessories	Under bed in front bedroom
MMB005	Green rifle case containing: Windsor 20 aa S. gun over and under, ser# 116661	Under bed in front bedroom
MMB006	Vanguard Weatherby rifle .270 cal ser# VL23514	Under bed in front bedroom
MMB007	Rossi .22 cal pump rifle ser# G429157	Under bed in front bedroom
PLF002	Calendar, plant date 3-13-94	Hanging on wall of porch
PLF003	Ruger Blackhawk .357 revolver w/ case S#37-07349	Above window on west wall on shelf of porch
MMB008	Remington 11-87 12 ga s. gun Factory handcase S# PC188034	Under bed in front bedroom
PLF004	Smith and Wesson 357 mag Mod 686 w/ case S# AYS8278	Above window on west wall on shelf off porch
MMB009	Remington 12 ga s. gun 870	Under bed in front

	Wingmaster w/ case S# N4475304 (CH DL)	bedroom
PLF005	Financial records in black box	South wall of porch
PLF006	Financial records in grey box	South wall of porch
PLF007	Financial records	South wall of porch
PLF008	Papers/ misc. w/ another person's name	South wall of porch
MMB010	Plastic seal-a-meal bag w/ marij 3 total	Closet in master Bedroom (front)
MMB011	Plastic baggie (Ziploc) (4) w/ marij residue	Floor by bed in master bedroom
MMB012	Sony video 8 camera w/ film and case s# 3060964	
PLF009	Red metal box w/ power ramset Tool	Porch next to door
PLF010	Misc. paper & warranties	S. wall of porch
PLF011	Medical prescriptions & receipts	S. wall on shelf—porch
PLF012	Grow receipts & warranties for grow equip, misc. papers w/ U-Hand receipts	S. wall on shelf—porch
PLF013	Realistic 2-way CB radio Bose Station s# 423494	E. wall on shelf—porch
PLF014	10 bullets, 3 speed loader, case, Wooden handle	Shelf on W. wall above window—porch
PLF015	9" approx. Bowie knife Pakistan	E wall hanging
PLF016	Photographs of marijuana	W. wall, shelf--window
PLF017	Food saver bags (box of), Makita recharger, Makita flashlight	S. wall above fridge W. wall shelf/N. wall porch
PLF018	2 marijuana grow books	Shelf on S. wall-porch
PLF019	Misc. paper work of Domicile	Mail bin on N. wall
PLF020	Cardboard drawer containing Receipts	S. wall shelf—porch
PLF021	Address book & 2 business cards	S. wall shelf—porch
MMB013	Ledger book	Shelf-master bedroom
PLF022	Compressor Nebulizer System	S. side of porch
PLF023	Norelco Clean Air System	S. wall—porch
PLF024	American Harvest Food Dehydrator	S. wall—porch
PLF025	Misc. papers and receipts	Front passenger area-Red Dodge OR RNN98
PLF026	Paper bag w/ marij plant (male)	Shelf on S. wall
PLF027	Film canister w/ small male marij	E. wall on frame-door
PLF028	Magazines for rifles (Ruger .22 w/ bullets, 223 w/ empty shells	On top of refrigerator on porch
PLF029	4 mini Cripple Creek P.D. badges, 2 papers: 1 map, 1 drawn	Box on mid-lower shelf—porch

MMB014	Sony camcorder box w/ Warranties	Storage under seat in Dining area
MMB015	Post-it note w/ address & phone #, roll of 35mm film	Kitchen counter
PLF030	Marij seeds in film canister	Shelf by window-porch
PLF031	Misc. papers, grow supplies, Telephone book w/ names	Shelf on S. wall-porch
PLF032	Radio shack portable CB s# 0041172	Top shelf/S. wall-Porch
MMB016	Stihl model F576 Brush cutter s# 24965931	Under porch on trailer
PLF033	4 marij plants & 1 pot (black plastic)	S of trailer approx. 200 yds.
DLL-021	One bayonet w/ sheath US M8A1	Top shelf on porch, above window

Chapter 2
Stop A Trial From Happening by Coping A Plea

SUMMARY OF COURT DOCUMENTS THAT FOLLOW

Mr. Patterson was not eligible for court appointed counsel.

Defendant was advised of his right to a jury trial/hearing and confrontation privilege against self-incrimination, and all other procedures and penalties required by law.

Counsel for defendant waived reading of accusatory instrument and acknowledged receipt of a certified true copy.

The district attorney, (Judge), reads the indictment/information/ fugitive complaint to the defendant and delivers a true copy to the defendant.

On October 18, 1994, Paul Jonah Patterson was indicted on counts 1, 7, and 13.

The above case was given a preliminary hearing on October 19, 1994, at 8:30 A.M.

The following arrangements were made for the release of the defendant:

Defendant to be held in custody and security is set at $250,000.00. This figure changes ultimately to $100,000.00.

FOR THE COUNTY OF ADAMS

THE STATE OF COLORADO   RECORD OF PROCEEDINGS
           Plaintiff   AND ORDER
   vs.

<u>Paul Jonah Patterson</u>   Case No. 94CR1763
        Defendant
_____
      True Name

The following proceedings were held in the above-captioned case before the undersigned judge on <u>10-13-94</u>.

_____D. Kentzer_____ District Attorney appearing for the State

(X) Arraignment/New Charge/Continued/DA Info/Detainer/Fugitive Complaint
( ) Arraignment-Probation Violation/Contempt/RO Violation/Diversion Violation
( ) Defendant failed to appear. B/W ordered, Security/Bail set $_____.
( ) Other _____

( ) Defendant appeared with counsel _____
(X) Defendant appeared without counsel, was informed of right to retained or appointed counsel and the court appointed not eligible for court-appointed counsel/continued proceedings to _____ so defendant could retain counsel.
( ) Defendant waived rights to counsel.

(X) Defendant advised of right to jury trial/hearing and confrontation, privilege against self-incrimination, and all other procedures and penalties required by law.

( ) Counsel for defendant waived reading of accusatory instrument, acknowledged receipt of a certified true copy.
(X) The Court ( ) district attorney, read the indictment/information/ fugitive complaint to the defendant/delivered a certified true copy to the defendant.

( ) Defendant waived Identity Hearing/Writ of Habeas Corpus/Extradition and signed a waiver and the court ordered defendant be held _____ days.

( ) Defendant ordered to report to jail forthwith to be booked and released.
( ) Defendant entered a plea of ( ) Not Guilty ( ) Guilty ( ) Divert ( ) No Contest ( ) Admitted Probation Violation to the following charges:
_____

( ) Other: _____
( ) Pay $ _____ By _____ and balance at $_____ Month
beginning _____ Or appear at 9AM next Judicial Day.

(X) THE ABOVE CASE HAS BEEN GIVEN A DAY AND TIME
CERTIFICATION FOR:
     PV/Omni/Identity/Preliminary/Extradition/RO 10-19-94 at 8:30 AM
     Writ of Habeas Corpus/Contempt of Court: _____ at _____
     Plea: _____ at _____. Sentencing: _____ at _____

Trial: _____ at _____
PSI: ( ) Requested ( ) Waived ( ) Further Time Waved
Other: _____
( ) Cancel date of: _____.
( ) _____ Dismissed Pursuant to Plea bargain.

The following arrangements were made for the release of the defendant:
( ) Release on own recognizance   ( ) Security set at $ 250,000.00
( ) Defendant held in custody   ( ) Bail set at $ _____

Dated 10-13-94   Reporter Betsy Barrett _____ Robert Walberg _____
                                             District/Circuit Judge

STATE OF COLORADO [] District Court
Adams County   [] Circuit Court

Case No. _____   VERIFICATION RECOMMENDATION RE:
                                    REQUEST FOR COURT-APPOINTED COUNSEL;

_____   ORDER APPOINTING OR DENYING COUNSEL

Charge(s): _____

_____

Case Name:

VERIFICATION RECOMMENDATION RE: REQUEST FOR COURT-APOINTED COUNSEL

(To be completed by Verification Specialist)

Based on the Affidavit of Indigence and Request for Court-Appointed Counsel, it is respectfully recommended that Defendant's request for a court-appointed attorney be:

[] APPROVED.
[] DENIED.
[] CONTINUED for _____ weeks for verification and information.
[] NO RECOMMENDATION.

_____   _____
DATE   VERIFICATION SPECIALIST

_____   _____
TELEPHONE NUMBER   PRINT OR TYPE NAME OF VERIFICATION SPECIALIST

_____

ORDER APPOINTING OR DENYING COUNSEL

(To be completed by Judge)

[] The court APPROVES defendant's request for court-appointed counsel.

_____ is hereby appointed by the court as attorney for Defendant, contingent upon verification. The compensation rate for noncontract-appointed counsel is at the current rate, absent authorization from the State Court Administrator for a higher rate.

[x] The court DENIES defendant's request for court-appointed counsel.

_____   _____
DATE   JUDGE

_____   _____
JUDGE'S O.S.B. NUMBER   PRINT, TYPE, OR STAMP NAME OF JUDGE

IN THE DISTRICT COURT FOR THE STATE COLORADO
COUNTY OF ADAMS

STATE OF COLORADO

    vs.

CASE NO. 94CR-1763____

Paul Patterson_____

_____

Address:_____

CHARGES: Multiple drug
Felon poss

_____

Employer: _____

_____

COMMENTS: Substantial priors of similar type in CA.

SUM OF 250,000

_____Andrew Levin_____

Release
Andrew
Levin
Circuit D J
Robert F. Walberg

RELEASE ASSISTANCE OFFICER

DATE: 10-13-94

____R. F. Walberg_____
CIRCUIT/DISTRICT JUDGE

**IN THE DISTRICT COURT FOR THE STATE OF COLORADO
FOR THE COUNTY OF ADAMS**

THE STATE OF COLORADO   RECORD OF PROCEEDINGS
           Plaintiff   AND ORDER

     vs.

Paul Jonah Patterson   Case No. 94CR1763
        Defendant

_____
       True Name

The following proceedings were held in the above-captioned case before the
undersigned judge on 10-19-94.

_____Paul Frasier_____ District Attorney appearing for the State

(X) Arraignment/New Charge/Continued/DA Info/Detainer/Fugitive Complaint
( ) Arraignment-Probation Violation/Contempt/RO Violation/Diversion Violation
( ) Defendant failed to appear. B/W ordered, Security/Bail set $_____.
( ) Other _____

( ) Defendant appeared with counsel __Michael Lehman_____
(X) Defendant appeared without counsel, was informed of right to retained or
appointed counsel and the court appointed not eligible for court-appointed
counsel/continued proceedings to _____ so defendant could
retain counsel.
( ) Defendant waived rights to counsel.

( ) Defendant advised of right to jury trial/hearing and confrontation, privilege
against self-incrimination, and all other procedures and penalties required by law.

( ) Counsel for defendant waived reading of accusatory instrument, acknowledged
receipt of a certified true copy.
( ) The Court ( ) district attorney, read the indictment/information/ fugitive
complaint to the defendant/delivered a certified true copy to the defendant.

( ) Defendant waived Identity Hearing/Writ of Habeas Corpus/Extradition and
signed a waiver and the court ordered defendant be held _____ days.

( ) Defendant ordered to report to jail forthwith to be booked and released.
( ) Defendant entered a plea of ( ) Not Guilty ( ) Guilty ( ) Divert ( ) No Contest (
) Admitted Probation Violation to the following charges:
_____

( ) Other: _____
( ) Pay $ _____ By _____ and balance at $_____ Month
beginning _____ Or appear at 9AM next Judicial Day.

(X) THE ABOVE CASE HAS BEEN GIVEN A DAY AND TIME
CERTIFICATION FOR:
    PV/Omni/Identity/Preliminary/Extradition/RO 10-19-94 at 8:30 AM

Writ of Habeas Corpus/Contempt of Court: _____ at _____
Plea: <u>11-9-94</u> at <u>9:00</u>. Sentencing: _____ at _____

Trial: _____ at _____
    PSI: ( ) Requested ( ) Waived ( ) Further Time Waved
    Other: <u> Bail Hearing 10/31/94 @ 9:00   </u>
( ) Cancel date of: _____.
( ) _____ Dismissed Pursuant to Plea bargain.

The following arrangements were made for the release of the defendant:
( ) Release on own recognizance   ( ) Security set at $ 250,000.00
( ) Defendant held in custody   ( ) Bail set at $ _____

Dated 10-19-94   Reporter <u>T. Gardner</u>   _____<u>Richard Barron</u>_____
                                         District/Circuit Judge

DANIEL HINRICHS
ATTORNEY AT LAW

590 Commercial   Office (503) 267-0229
Adams, Colorado 97420   Fax (503) 267-0154

October 20, 1994

Circuit Court Clerk, Criminal
Adams County Courthouse
Cripple Creek, Colorado 97423

Re: State of Colorado v. Teresa Patterson
    Case No. 94 CR 1763

Dear Clerk:

Please note for the record that I have been retained by Ms. Patterson to represent her in the above referenced matter.

If you have any questions please feel free to contact my office.

Sincerely,

Daniel M. Hinrichs

DMH: tmr

cc: Teresa Patterson
    District Attorney

IN THE CIRCUIT COURT OF THE STATE OF COLORADO
FOR THE COUNTY OF ADAMS

STATE OF COLORADO,

Case No. 94CR1763

Plaintiff

vs.

REQUEST FOR RELEASE REVIEW

Paul Jonah Patterson

Defendant

_____

Defendant by and through his attorney, Michael R. Lehman, hereby moves the court to review the release status of the Defendant and to consider the Defendant's release on personal recognizance or, in the alternative, on conditional release, or, in the alternative, on a reduced financial deposit.

Defendant requests evidentiary hearing and oral argument on this request.

Dated this __20__ day of ___October___, 1994.

Michael R. Lehman [78282]
Attorney for Defendant

AUTHORITES

COS 135.220
COS 135.245
COS 135.285(1)

Liberman v. Burfs, 293 Or. 457 (1982)

CERTIFICATE OF MAILING

I certify that I served the foregoing

REQUEST FOR RELEASE REVIEW

on the below named persons by depositing a true, full and exact copy thereof in the United States Post Office at Adams,, Colorado, on October 20, 1994, enclosed in a sealed envelope, with postage paid, addressed to:

District Attorney's Office
Adams County Courthouse
Cripple Creek, Colorado 97423

Michael R. Lehman [78282]
Attorney for Defendant

IN THE CIRCUIT COURT OF THE STATE OF COLORADO
FOR THE COUNTY OF ADAMS

STATE OF COLORADO,
                Plaintiff
  vs.

Paul J. Patterson
                Defendant

RELEASE HEARING REPORT

Case No. 94CR-1763

Charge: CMCS/MCS; CDCS/DCS; CPCS/PCS;
        Child Neglect I (3); Endangering
        Minor (3); Felon Poss/Firearms (12)

SRA/ROR Recommended: $150,000.00-Reduced $100,000 (10-31-94)

The defendant is 39 years old. He has lived in Adams County for approximately three years during which time he was employed by the cities of Gold Mine and Cripple Creek as a building inspector. This employment has apparently been terminated. He previously resided in Salem, Colorado for about two years where he went to school for retraining following an injury sustained while working in construction. He came to Salem form Monterey, California. If released he would continue to reside in Cripple Creek and help arrange for his family's stability during the time he expects to be serving in prison.

According to criminal records, the defendant was first arrested in California in 1975 and convicted of Receiving Stolen Property. He had arrests in 1976 and 1977 for drugs and car stealing, both of which were dismissed. In 1977 he was convicted of PCS and placed on probation. While incarcerated in 1978 he was charged with PCS in a jail facility and convicted of that charge. His probation was violated, but he was continued on probation for both convictions. In 1980 he was arrested for Cultivation of Marijuana and Assault with a Deadly Weapon. Following a plea bargain, he pled to a Battery charge. His probations were revoked in December, 1980, and he was sentenced to prison. He was paroled in December of 1981. In 1983, he was again convicted of Cultivation of Marijuana and placed on probation. He states he moved to Colorado soon after completing that probation.

The present charges resulted from the service of a search warrant at the residence of the defendant and his wife. Discovered was a substantial marijuana growing operation in the process of being prepared for harvest and shipment. In addition to the marijuana, the defendant's three children were at the residence as well as numerous firearms. The defendant's wife, Teresa Patterson, is also charged and has been ROR'd.

This defendant has a significant history of similar conduct, although he has not been caught at it for the past 10 years. In view of his prior record and the substantial nature of this operation, with the high probability of a prison sentence, security should be required in an amount commensurate with the circumstances.

Andrew Levin, Release Assistance Officer

October 26, 1994

IN THE CIRCUIT COURT FOR THE STATE OF COLORADO
FOR THE COUNTY OF ADAMS

THE STATE OF COLORADO   RECORD OF PROCEEDINGS
                        Plaintiff   AND ORDER
   vs.

Paul Jonah Patterson   Case No. 94CR1763
      Defendant

_____
      True Name

The following proceedings were held in the above-captioned case before the undersigned judge on 10-31-94.

_____Paul Frasier_____ District Attorney appearing for the State

( ) Arraignment/New Charge/Continued/DA Info/Detainer/Fugitive Complaint
( ) Arraignment-Probation Violation/Contempt/RO Violation/Diversion Violation
( ) Defendant failed to appear. B/W ordered, Security/Bail set $_____.
(X) Other _Release Hearing_____

(X) Defendant appeared with counsel __Michael Lehman_____
( ) Defendant appeared without counsel, was informed of right to retained or appointed counsel and the court appointed not eligible for court-appointed counsel/continued proceedings to _____ so defendant could retain counsel.
( ) Defendant waived rights to counsel.

( ) Defendant advised of right to jury trial/hearing and confrontation, privilege against self-incrimination, and all other procedures and penalties required by law.

( ) Counsel for defendant waived reading of accusatory instrument, acknowledged receipt of a certified true copy.
( ) The Court ( ) district attorney, read the indictment/information/ fugitive complaint to the defendant/delivered a certified true copy to the defendant.

( ) Defendant waived Identity Hearing/Writ of Habeas Corpus/Extradition and signed a waiver and the court ordered defendant be held _____ days.

( ) Defendant ordered to report to jail forthwith to be booked and released.
( ) Defendant entered a plea of ( ) Not Guilty ( ) Guilty ( ) Divert ( ) No Contest
( )Admitted Probation Violation to the following charges:

_____

(X) Other: ___Court reduced_____
( ) Pay $ _____ By _____ and balance at $_____ Month
beginning _____ Or appear at 9AM next Judicial Day.

(X) THE ABOVE CASE HAS BEEN GIVEN A DAY AND TIME
CERTIFICATION FOR:
   PV/Omni/Identity/Preliminary/Extradition/RO 10-19-94 at 8:30 AM

Writ of Habeas Corpus/Contempt of Court: _____ at _____
Plea: 11-9-94 at 9:00. Sentencing: _____ at _____

Trial: _____ at _____
    PSI: ( ) Requested ( ) Waived ( ) Further Time Waved
    Other: _Bail Hearing 10/31/94 @ 9:00_____
( ) Cancel date of: _____.
( ) _____ Dismissed Pursuant to Plea bargain.

The following arrangements were made for the release of the defendant:
( ) Release on own recognizance   ( ) Security set at $ <u>Now 100,000.00</u>
( ) Defendant held in custody   ( ) Bail set at $ _____

Dated <u>10-31-94</u> Reporter <u>Phyllis Campbell</u> _____<u>Richard Barron</u>_____
                                                         District/Circuit Judge

IN THE CIRCUIT COURT OF THE STATE OF COLORADO
FOR ADAMS COUNTY

STATE OF COLORADO

        PLAINTIFF,   No. 94-CR-1763

   vs.

PAUL J. PATTERSON   PLAINTIFF'S MOTION TO
                                 CONSOLIDATE
        DEFENDANT

    COMES NOW R. Paul Frasier, Forfeiture Counsel for Adams County, Colorado and respectfully moves to consolidating this matter with the lawsuit now pending in Adams County for the purpose of avoiding any charges that Paul J. Patterson in either of these cases has.

    Dated this 14th day of October, 1994.

****
    IT IS HEREBY ORDERED that the move to consolidate these matters is hereby

    ____ALLOWED

   _X_DENIED

Dated this 31st day of October, 1994.

                      ____Richard Barron_____
                      Circuit Judge

****

I certify that I served a true copy of this document on Mike Lehman, attorney for the defendant. In compliance with the applicable rules of the Colorado Rules of Civil Procedure on the 14th day of October, 1994.

R. Paul Frasier OSB # 84223
Forfeiture Counsel

IN THE CIRCUIT COURT OF THE STATE OF COLORADO
FOR THE COUNTY OF ADAMS

STATE OF COLORADO
              Plaintiff,   Case No. 94CR1763

vs.

                                PETITION TO ENTER PLEA OF
Paul J. Patterson   GUILTY AND ORDER ENTERING
             Defendant   PLEA

1. My full true name is __Paul J. Patterson____, and I am (x) am not ( ) an American citizen. I understand that if I am not an American citizen I can be deported form the United States, excluded from admission to the United States, or denied naturalization as an American citizen.

2. I am represented by a lawyer whose name is Michael R. Lehman.

3. I have received a copy of the accusatory instrument filed against me.

4. I wish to plead guilty to the charge(s) of: Manufacture of controlled substance/Felon in poss of firearm/Child Neglect.

____(a) Class A Felony:

____(b) Felony seriously endangering life/safety of another:

____(c) Other crimes: _____

5. I know if I plead guilty to the charged, the maximum possible sentence is _35_ years imprisonment and/or a fine of $300,000. I know also that the sentence is up to the court only.

6. I have (x) have not ( ) been convicted of one or more felonies in the past as follows: _____

_____

7. I also know if I am pleading guilty to felony that seriously endangered the life/safety of another and I have a prior felony conviction or I am pleading guilty to a class A felony, it may be decided I am a dangerous offender and the maximum sentence may be increased to 30 years for each such charge.

8. I am ( ) am not (x) presently on probation or parole. I understand that by pleading guilty in this case my probation or parole may be revoked. I further understand that if my parole or probation is revoked, any sentence in that case may be consecutive to or in addition to any sentence in this case.

9. I understand that by pleading guilty I give up my right to have a jury trial and agree that a judge alone can decide my case. I know a jury has 12 citizens of Adams County on it and it takes 10 out of 12 to find me guilty or not guilty.

10. I understand that by pleading guilty I give up my right to confront the witnesses against me. I knew this means that I do not get to see, hear and question the witnesses against me in court. I know that no witnesses are necessary because I am pleading guilty.

11. I understand that by pleading guilty I give up my privilege as...know this means I will have to...if I pleaded not guilty, I...not say anything about the...would not be used against me.

12. I understand...will not be necessary for the ...reasonable doubt and I also know...will no longer be presumed to be ...which I am charged.

13. I understand that by pleading guilty I can only appeal to a...the judge gives me. I know that...to complain to a higher court...the police, the prosecution, my...

14. I...FREELY AND VOLUNTARILY AND OF MY OWN ACCORD AND WITH FULL UNDERSTANDING OF ALL THE MATTERS SET FORTH IN THE INDICTMENT ( ) INFORMATION ( ) AND THIS PETITION.

15. I request the court to enter my plea of "Guilty".

SIGNED by me in open court this _9_ day of _November_, 1994.

_____Paul Patterson_____
Defendant

Witness: _____Michael R. Lehman_____
          Attorney for Defendant

ORDER

IT IS ORDERED that the defendant's plea of "GUILTY" be accepted and entered as prayed for in the petition.

Done in open court this _9_ day of _Nov._, 1994.

_____Richard Barron_____
Circuit Court Judge

IN THE CIRCUIT COURT OF THE STATE OF COLORADO
FOR THE COUNTY OF ADAMS

THE STATE OF COLORADO   RECORD OF PROCEEDINGS
           Plaintiff   AND ORDER

    vs.

Paul Jonah Patterson   Case No. 94CR1763
       Defendant

_____
       True Name

The following proceedings were held in the above-captioned case before the undersigned judge on <u>11-9-94</u>.

        _____<u>Paul Frasier</u>_____ District Attorney appearing for the State

(X) Arraignment/New Charge/Continued/DA Info/Detainer/Fugitive Complaint
( ) Arraignment-Probation Violation/Contempt/RO Violation/Diversion Violation
( ) Defendant failed to appear. B/W ordered, Security/Bail set $_____.
( ) Other _____

(X) Defendant appeared with counsel __<u>Michael Lehman</u>_____
( ) Defendant appeared without counsel, was informed of right to retained or appointed counsel and the court appointed not eligible for court-appointed counsel/continued proceedings to _____ so defendant could retain counsel.
( ) Defendant waived rights to counsel.

( ) Defendant advised of right to jury trial/hearing and confrontation, privilege against self-incrimination, and all other procedures and penalties required by law.

( ) Counsel for defendant waived reading of accusatory instrument, acknowledged receipt of a certified true copy.
( ) The Court ( ) district attorney, read the indictment/information/ fugitive complaint to the defendant/delivered a certified true copy to the defendant.

( ) Defendant waived Identity Hearing/Writ of Habeas Corpus/Extradition and signed a waiver and the court ordered defendant be held _____ days.

(X) Defendant ordered to report to jail forthwith to be booked and released.
( ) Defendant entered a plea of ( ) Not Guilty (X) Guilty ( ) Divert ( ) No Contest
( ) Admitted Probation Violation to the following charges: ____ <u>2, 7, &</u>
<u>13</u>_____

( ) Other: _____
( ) Pay $ _____ By _____ and balance at $_____ Month
beginning _____ Or appear at 9AM next Judicial Day.

(X) THE ABOVE CASE HAS BEEN GIVEN A DAY AND TIME
CERTIFICATION FOR:
    PV/Omni/Identity/Preliminary/Extradition/RO 10-19-94 at 8:30 AM

Writ of Habeas Corpus/Contempt of Court: _____ at _____
Plea: 11-9-94 at 9:00. Sentencing: _11/14/94_ at _9:00_.
Trial: _____ at _____
    PSI: ( ) Requested ( ) Waived ( ) Further Time Waved
    Other: _Bail Hearing 10/31/94 @ 9:00_____
( ) Cancel date of: _____.
( ) _____ Dismissed Pursuant to Plea bargain.

The following arrangements were made for the release of the defendant:
( ) Release on own recognizance   ( ) Security set at $ 250,000.00
( ) Defendant held in custody   ( ) Bail set at $ _____

Dated 11-9-94 Reporter <u>Kay Marino</u>   _____<u>Richard Barron_____</u>
                                              District/Circuit Judge

IN THE CIRCUIT COURT OF THE STATE OF COLORADO FOR THE COUNTY OF ADAMS

STATE OF COLORADO   Case No. 94CR1763

      v.

Paul Jonah Patterson
Defendant

                       (x)Judgment of Conviction/Sentence
                       ( ) Order on Probation Violation/Sentence

The above named Defendant coming before this court on <u>11-14-94</u>, the State appearing by <u>Paul Frasier</u>, Assistant District Attorney; Defendant appearing in person and by attorney <u>Michael Lehman;</u> Defendant being advised of the right to counsel and pled: <u>GUILTY</u> and is convicted of the following offenses.

Case/Count	Offense
2	MANUFACTURE CONTROLLED SUBSTANCE- Marijuana
7	CHILD NEGLECT I
13	FELON IN POSSESSION OF FIREARM

IT IS HEREBY ORDERED:

1.___**DRUG DIVERSION**-Defendant's guilty plea to PCS _____ is accepted
        Under COS 475.245
___an adjudication of guilt ( ) shall not be ( ) is entered at this time

2.___Counts dismissed: _____
     ___ Cases dismissed: _____

3.___ Presentence report ( ) received ( ) waived

4.___ **DEFENDANT IS SENTENCED TO:**
     _____ days/months Adams County Jail
     _____On Ct. 2—MFG CS—Marij_____
   _X_ 26 months Department of Corrections; followed by _36_ months
        post-prison supervision
   ___ pay fines, costs, fees, assessments, restitution as set forth in the
        Money Judgment section below
   ___ _____ months for Dangerous Offender _____ months gun minimum
   ___ early release for residential drug/alcohol treatment

5. _X_ **PROBATION:** On Ct. 7 and 13
   _X_ sentenced to probation for _36_ months _____ to the:
     _x_ Department of Corrections (see attached sheet for conditions).
     ___ Court (see attached sheet for conditions).
   ___ Court finds jail space available and imposes: _____sanction units
effective ( ) immediately ( ) beginning on _____, at _____ AM/PM
   ___ early release for drug/alcohol residential treatment

_____ _____hours community service work to be completed by _____

_____ comply with previously imposed conditions of probation

_x_ serve _90_ days in the Adams County jail effective on each charge, to sentence and consecutively to each other. –NO CREDIT.

6.____ **OTHER ORDERS**: _____

_____

MONEY JUDGMENT

Case/Count
94CR1763

Amount
_____

_____ | _____

_____ | _____

Judgment Creditor: State of Colorado   Total Judgment Amount $ 1,000.00

Judgment Debtor: Paul Jonah Patterson   SSN _____

UNAS $ 282.00 FINE $ 659.00 OPTS $ _____ REST $ _____ COMP $ _____

ATFE $ _____ DICO $ _____ COST $ _____ CJAS $ 54.00 LEML $ 5.00

Restitution:

Name and Address   Amount

   1. _____ $ _____

_____

_____

   2. _____

_____

_____

   3. _____

_____

_____

PAYMENT TERMS:
____ Immediately due
_x_ at $ 100.00 per month, beginning _30_ days
____ bail or security is applied
____ restitution joint and several with _____ in Case No. _____
____ report to court at 9:00 AM the next judicial day if your payment is not
made in full as ordered
____ to be set by court collections officer
____ other: _____

Payable to:

STATE COURT ACCOUNTING, ADAMS COUNTY COURTHOUSE, CRIPPLE CREEK, OR
97423

Dated this 16th day of November, 1994

Reporter: Kay Marino

                       Richard Barron
Interpreter: _____   Circuit/District Judge

IN THE CIRCUIT COURT FOR THE STATE OF COLORADO
FOR ADAMS COUNTY

STATE OF COLORADO
        Plaintiff,
        vs.

Paul Jonah Patterson
Teresa M. Patterson
        Defendants.

Case No. 94CR1756
       94CR1763
       94CR2156

SATISFACTION OF
MONEY JUDGMENT

STATE OF COLORADO   )
) ss
County of Adams   )

Plaintiff acknowledges satisfaction of the amounts stated in the Money Judgment made and docketed in the above-entitles court and cause.

Dated on April 26th, 1995.

                               PAUL R. BURGETT
                               District Attorney for Adams
County

                               Adams County Courthouse
                               Cripple Creek, OR 97423

                               By: __Paul R. Burgett_

Subscribed and sworn to before me on April 26th, 1995

                               __Laurie K. Kreutzer_____
                               NOTARY PUBLIC FOR COLORADO

                               My Commission Expires: 10-14-97

CERTIFICATE OF SERVICE BY MAIL

I certify that on April 26th. 1995 I served the foregoing Satisfaction of Money Judgment upon the defendants hereto by mailing, regular mail, postage prepaid, a true, exact and full copy thereof to:

Ticor Title Company
P.O. Box 368
Cripple Creek, OR 97423

                               R. Paul Frasier
                               District Attorney/Assistant
                               Adams County Courthouse
                                 Cripple Creek, OR 97423

IN THE CIRCUIT COURT OF THE STATE OF COLORADO FOR THE COUNTY OF ADAMS

STATE OF COLORADO   Case No. 94CR1763
v.
PAUL JONAH PATTERSON
Defendant.

(X)Judgment of Conviction/Sentence
( ) Order on Probation Violation/ Sentence

The above named Defendant coming before this court on 11-14-94, the State appearing by Paul Frasier, Assistant District Attorney; Defendant appearing in person and by attorney Michael Lehman; Defendant being advised of the right to counsel; pled GUILTY to and is convicted of the following offenses.

Case/Count	Offense
2	**MANUFACTURE CONTROLLED SUBSTANCE- Marijuana**
7	**CHILD NEGLECT I**
13	**FELON IN POSSESSION OF FIREARM**

IT IS HEREBY ORDERED:

1. ___**DRUG DIVERSION-** Defendant's guilty plea to PCS _____ is accepted. Under COS 475.245
___an adjudication of guilt ( ) shall not be ( ) is entered at this time
2. ___Counts dismissed: _____
___Cases dismissed: _____
3. ___Presentence report ( ) received ( ) waived
4. _X_ **DEFENDANT IS SENTENCED TO:**
___ _____ days/months Adams County Jail
___ On Ct. 2—MFG CS-Marij.
_x_ 26 months Department of Corrections; followed by _36_ months post-prison supervision
___ pay fines, costs, fees, assessments, restitution as set forth in the Money Judgment section below
___ _____ months Dangerous Offended _____ months gun minimum
___ early release for residential drug/alcohol treatment
5. _X_**PROBATION:** On Ct. 7 and 13
_x_ sentenced to probation for _36_ months to the:
_x_ Department of Corrections (see attached sheet for conditions)
___Court (see attached sheet for conditions)
___Court finds jail space available and imposes: ___sanction units effective ( ) immediately ( ) beginning on _____, at _____AM/PM
___early release for drug/alcohol treatment
___ _____ hours community service work to be completed by _____
___ comply with previously imposed conditions of probation
_x_ serve _90_ days in the Adams County Jail effective on each charge, to run consecutively to the above prison sentence and consecutively to each other. –NO CREDIT
6. ___**OTHER ORDERS:** _____

IN THE CIRCUIT/DISTRICT COURT OF THE STATE OF COLORADO
FOR COOS COUNTY

ADAMS COUNTY
Plaintiff

**NOTICE OF DISMISSAL AND
JUDGMENT**

vs.

REAL PROPERTY, 2755 SHELLEY RD.,   Case No. 94CV1067
CRIPPLE CREEK
Defendant

there having been no service of petition or summons upon the defendant;

having not pleaded within the time allowed by law or Order of the Court;

there having been no activity in the above entitled cause as reflected by the file for 90 days;

the above entitled cause has been put on the record as being fully compromised and settled;

the time for appeal has expired;

XX other: Case having settled:

_____

IT IS THEREFORE ORDERED:
XX The above entitled matter is dismissed on the 28th day after the date of this Order unless an appropriate Order or Judgment is filed or good cause is shown by Motion and Affidavit;

That the exhibits be disposed of unless the parties make arrangements for their release within 28 days.

Dated this 28th day of Dec. in Cripple Creek, Colorado.

____Richard Barron_____
Circuit Court Judge

Cc: Circuit Court Judge
    Richard Barron

IN THE CIRCUIT/DISTRICT COURT OF THE STATE OF COLORADO
FOR COOS COUNTY
250 N. Baxter, Cripple Creek, Colorado 97423
503/396-3121 ext. 259

January 10, 1995

Robert Paul Frasier
Attorney at Law
SPECIAL NARCOTICS PROSECUTOR   Bar #: 84223
1975 MC PHERSON ROOM 302
NORTH BEND OR 97459

Adams County/ Real Property 2755 Shelley
Case #:   94CV1067   Civil Forfeiture

NOTICE OF SCHEDULED COURT PROCEEDING

Scheduled Proceeding: Request Trial Date
Date: 1/25/95
Room:
Additional Information:
   MARCH, APRIL,
   MAY, JUNE

The parties must agree upon a trial day under UTCR 7.020. The court prefers the trial date be within the months listed above. The Court must receive three possible agreed upon dates in writing by the above date. Indicate the length of trial and whether a jury is requested. Jury trials will not be set on Fridays unless four days or more are needed or on Mondays unless five days or more are needed. If the parties cannot agree on a date, they must immediately request a conference with the Presiding Judge.

IF DATES ARE NOT RECEIVED OR A CONFERENCE DOES NOT OCCUR   BEFORE THE ABOVE DATE THE COURT WILL SET A ONE DAY TRIAL AT ITS CONVENIENCE.

Client (s) of Addressee:
Adams County

CC:
Real Property 2755 Shelley Rd
Teresa M. Patterson
Michael R Lehman

IN THE CIRCUIT/DISTRICT COURT OF THE STATE OF COLORADO
FOR COOS COUNTY

ADAMS COUNTY, a political
   Subdivision of the State of
   Colorado,

      Plaintiff,   Case No. 94-CV-1067

      V.

Paul J. Patterson, Teresa M.   NOTICE OF PENDENCY
Patterson AND THE REAL   OF ACTION
PROPERTY LOCATED AT 2755
SHELLEY ROAD, CRIPPLE CREEK,
ADAMS COUNTY, COLORADO
   Defendant

Notice is hereby given that pursuant to COS 93.740, the undersigned

states:

1. As plaintiff, Adams County, a political subdivision of the State of

   Colorado, has filed an action in the Circuit Court for Adams

   County, Colorado;

2. The defendant if more particularly described in Exhibit A;

3. The object of the action is the forfeiture and condemnation to

   Adams County, a political subdivision of the State of Colorado;

   and

                        After Recording Return To:
                        R. Paul Frasier
                        S.R.I.N.T.
                        1975 McPherson Room #302
                        North Bend, Colorado 97459

NOTICE OF PENDENCY OF AN ACTION

4. The description of the real property to be affected is as set forth

in Exhibit A, attached to this notice and by this reference

incorporated herein.

> R. PAUL FRASIER   #84223
> Forfeiture Counsel
> South River Interagency
>   Narcotics Team
> 1975 McPherson Room #302
> North Bend, Colorado 97459
> Telephone: (503 756-2020 ext. 576)

STATE OF COLORADO)
) ss.
COUNTY OF ADAMS   )

The foregoing instrument was acknowledged before me this 12th

day of October, 1994 by R. Paul Frasier.

>   Teri Sue Fresidden
> NOTARY PUBLIC FOR COLORADO
> My commission expires: 10-17-94

NOTICE OF PENDENCY OF AN ACTION

EXHIBIT A

The real property located at 2755 Shelley Road, Cripple Creek, Adams County, Colorado, Tax Account 8392.00, which is further described as being the east ½ of the west ½ of the southwest ¼ of the northwest ¼ of section 5, Township 28 South, Range 12 West of the Willamette Meridian, Adams County, Colorado, together with an Easement as set forth in an instrument recorded November 18, 1947, in Book 175, Page 400, Deed Records of Adams County, Colorado.

**IN THE CIRCUIT COURT OF THE STATE OF COLORADO
FOR THE COUNTY OF ADAMS**

ADAMS COUNTY, a political
    subdivision of the
    State of Colorado,
          Plaintiff,

    v.

THE REAL PROPERTY LOCATED
AT 2755 SHELLEY ROAD,
CRIPPLE CREEK, ADAMS COUNTY, COLORADO,
MORE PARTICULARLY DESCRIBED
IN THE ATTACHED EXHIBIT "A",

      Defendant.

Case # 94CV1067
COMPLAINT IN REM
FOR CIVIL
FORFEITURE UNDER HOUSE
BILL 2282, COLORADO
LAWS 1989, CHAPTER 791
JURY TRIAL REQUESTED

PLAINTIFF, ADAMS COUNTY, alleges as follows:

1.

Plaintiff, Adams County, is a political subdivision of the State of Colorado.

2.

Defendant is more particularly described in the attached exhibit A, which is incorporated by this reference herein.

3.

This court has jurisdiction over this action under HB 2282, Colorado Laws 1989, Chapter 791.

4.

On or about 10-12-94, in the area of Cripple Creek, County of Adams, State of Colorado, authorized agents of the South River Interagency Narcotics Team lawfully searched the defendant real property by means of a search warrant issued by the Adams County Colorado District Court. On or about 10-12-94, plaintiff filed a notice of lis pendens, thereby seizing defendant real property under the authority of Colorado Laws 1989, Chapter 791.

COUNT I:
As Count I, plaintiff alleges:

5.

The allegations of paragraphs 1-4 are adopted by this reference in this Count.

6.

Defendant is proceeds of or from prohibited conduct as defined in 1989 Colorado Laws, Chapter 791 in that between October 14, 1992 and October 12, 1994, in Adams County, Colorado, said defendant was purchased with, maintained with, preserved with, or otherwise supported with proceeds from the felony crimes of manufacture, delivery or possession of a controlled substance, to-wit: marijuana, or conspiracy to commit said crimes, which crimes were committed by Paul J. Patterson and Teresa M. Patterson, the potential claimants in this matter, and a person or persons unknown.

COUNT II

As Count II, plaintiff alleges:

7.

The allegations of paragraphs 1-4 are adopted by this reference in this Count.

8.

Defendants were used or were intended to be used to facilitate prohibited conduct as defined in 1989 Colorado Laws, Chapter 791 in that between October 14, 1992 and October 12, 1994, in Adams County, Colorado, said defendants were used or were intended to be used in the felony crimes of manufacture, delivery or possession of a controlled substance, to-wit: marijuana, or conspiracy to commit said crimes, which crimes were committed by Paul J. Patterson and Teresa M. Patterson, the potential claimants in this matter, and a person or persons unknown.

WHEREFORE, plaintiff, Adams County, prays that defendants be forfeited to the South River Interagency Narcotics Team, for its attorney fees, costs and disbursements and for such other and further relief as is just and equitable; and all right, title and interest pass to the plaintiff from the time of the prohibited conduct alleged herein, and that plaintiff and have such other and further relief as is just and equitable.

DATED this 12th day of October, 1994.

Respectfully submitted,

R. Paul Frasier
Forfeiture Counsel/OSB# 84223

EXHIBIT "A"

1) THE REAL PROPERTY LOCATED AT 2755 SHELLEY ROAD, CRIPPLE CREEK, ADAMS COUNTY, COLORADO, MORE PARTICULARLY DESCRIBED AS FOLLOWS:

   Tax Account 8392.00; the east ½ of the west ½ of the southwest ¼ of the northwest ¼ of section 5, Township 28 South, Range 12 West of the Willamette Meridian, Adams County, Colorado, together with an Easement as set forth in an instrument recorded November 18, 1947, in Book 175, Page 400, Deed Records of Adams County, Colorado.

IN THE CIRCUIT COURT OF THE STATE OF COLORADO
FOR ADAMS COUNTY

ADAMS COUNTY, COLORADO

        PLAINTIFF,   No. 94-CV-1067

vs.

THE REAL PROPERTY LOCATED   PLAINTIFF'S MOTION TO
AT 2755 SHELLEY ROAD,   CONSOLIDATE
CRIPPLE CREEK, ADAMS COUNTY,
COLORADO,

        DEFENDANT

COMES NOW R. Paul Frasier, Special Narcotics Prosecutor and Forfeiture Counsel for Adams County, Colorado and respectfully moves the Court for an Order consolidating this matter with the in the criminal case now pending in Adams County Circuit Court #94-CV-1067 for the purposes of avoiding any claim of double jeopardy by Paul J. Patterson in either of these proceedings.

Dated this 14th day of October, 1994.

                    R. Paul Frasier OSB #84223

IT IS HEREBY ORDERED that the plaintiff's motion to consolidate these matters is hereby:

        ____ALLOWED.
        ____DENIED.

Dated this ____ day of October, 1994.

                    Circuit Judge Richard Barron

SOUTH RIVER INTERAGENCY NARCOTICS TEAM
1975 MCPHERSON ROOM 302
DENVER, COLORADO 97459
503-756-2020 EXT 559

October 25, 1994
Paul Jonah Patterson
Teresa Matthews Patterson
2755 Shelley Road
Cripple Creek, Colorado 97423

It has come to my attention that you are harvesting the timber on the land located at 2755 Shelley Road, Cripple Creek, Colorado.

Please be advised that this property has been seized for forfeiture and a Les Pendence action has been filed and registered at the Adams County Clerk's Office. By harvesting the timber, you may be committing "waste" of the assets.

If you continue harvesting the timber or selling timber already down we will take every appropriate legal action to obtain an injunction, an accounting and requirements to pay any proceeds into court, or any other legal remedy available to this office.

S.H. Keutzer
Acting Forfeiture Counsel

SHK/kjs

IN THE CIRCUIT COURT OF THE STATE OF COLORADO
FOR THE COUNTY OF ADAMS

ADAMS COUNTY, a political
subdivision of the
State of Colorado,
      Plaintiff,

v.

THE REAL PROPERTY LOCATED
AT 2755 SHELLEY ROAD,
CRIPPLE CREEK, ADAMS COUNTY, COLORADO,
MORE PARTICULARLY DESCRIBED
IN THE ATTACHED EXHIBIT "A",
AND THE PERSONAL PROPERTY MORE
PARTICULARLY DESCRIBED IN THE
ATTACHED EXHIBIT "B",
      Defendants.

Case # 94CV1067

FIRST AMENDED
COMPLAINT IN REM
FOR CIVIL
FORFEITURE UNDER HOUSE
BILL 2282, COLORADO
LAWS 1989, CHAPTER 791
JURY TRIAL REQUESTED

PLAINTIFF, ADAMS COUNTY, alleges as follows:

1.

Plaintiff, Adams County, is a political subdivision of the State of Colorado.

2.

Defendants are more particularly described in the attached exhibit "A" and "B", which are incorporated by this reference herein.

3.

This court has jurisdiction over this action under HB 2282, Colorado Laws 1989, Chapter 791.

4.

On or about 10-12-94, in the area of Cripple Creek, County of Adams, State of Colorado, authorized agents of the South River Interagency Narcotics Team lawfully searched the defendant real property by means of a search warrant issued by the Adams County Colorado District Court. On or about 10-12-94, plaintiff filed a notice of lis pendens, thereby seizing defendant real property under the authority of Colorado Laws 1989, Chapter 791. The defendant personal property as described in exhibit "B" herein was seized during the execution of said search warrant on 10/12/94 pursuant to the authority of Colorado Laws 1989, Chapter 791.

COUNT I

As Count I, plaintiff alleges:

5.

The allegation of paragraphs 1-4 are adopted by this reference in this count.

6.

Defendants are proceeds of or from prohibited conducts as defined in the 1989 Colorado Laws, Chapter 791 in that between October 14, 1992 and October 12, 1994, in Adams County Colorado, said defendants were purchased with, maintained with, preserved with or otherwise supported with proceeds from the felony crimes of manufacture, delivery or possession of a controlled substance, to-wit: marijuana, or conspiracy to commit said crimes, which crimes were committed by Paul Jonah Patterson and Teresa Matthews Patterson, the potential claimants in this matter, and a person or persons unknown.

COUNT II

As Count II, plaintiff alleges:

7.

The allegation of paragraphs 1-4 are adopted by this reference in this count.

8.

Defendants were used or were intended to be used to facilitate prohibited conduct as defined in the 1989 Colorado Laws, Chapter 791 in that between October 14, 1992 and October 12, 1994, in Adams County Colorado, said defendants were used or were intended to be used in the felony crimes of manufacture, delivery or possession of a controlled substance, to-wit: marijuana, or conspiracy to commit said crimes, which crimes were committed by Paul Jonah Patterson and Teresa Matthews Patterson, the potential claimants in this matter, and a person or persons unknown.

WHEREFORE, plaintiff, Adams County, prays that defendants be forfeited to the South River Interagency Narcotics Team, for its attorney fees, costs and disbursements and for such other and further relief as is just and equitable; and all right, title and interest pass to the plaintiff from the time of the prohibited conduct alleged herein, and that plaintiff and have such other and further relief as is just and equitable.

DATED this 15th day of November, 1994.

Respectfully submitted,

R. Paul Frasier
Forfeiture Counsel/OSB 84223

EXHIBIT "A"

1) THE REAL PROPERTY LOCATED AT 2755 SHELLEY ROAD, CRIPPLE CREEK, ADAMS COUNTY, COLORADO, MORE PARTICULARLY DESCRIBED AS FOLLOWS:

Tax Account 8392.00; the east ½ of the west ½ of the southwest ¼ of the northwest ¼ of section 5, Township 28 South, Range 12 West of the Willamette Meridian, Adams County, Colorado, together with an Easement as set forth in an instrument recorded November 18, 1947, in Book 175, Page 400, Deed Records of Adams County, Colorado.

IN THE CIRCUIT COURT OF THE STATE OF COLORADO
FOR THE COUNTY OF ADAMS

ADAMS COUNTY, a political
    subdivision of the
    State of Colorado,   Case No. 94CV1067
    Plaintiff,

       v.   SUMMONS

REAL PROPERTY LOCATED AT
2755 SHELLEY ROAD, CRIPPLE CREEK,
ADAMS COUNTY, COLORADO,
    Defendant.

TO: Teresa M. Patterson
    2755 Shelley Road
    Cripple Creek, Colorado

You are hereby required to appear and defend the complaint filed against you in the above-entitled action within 30 days from the date of service on this summons upon you, and in case of your failure to do so, for want thereof, plaintiff, Adams County, will apply to the court for the relief demanded in the complaint.

NOTICE TO THE DEFENDANT: READ THESE PAPERS CAREFULLY!

You must "appear" in this case or the other side will win automatically. To "appear" you must file with the court a legal paper called a "motion" or "answer". The "motion" or "answer" must be given to the court clerk or administrator within 30 days along with the required filing fee. It must be in proper form and have proof of service on the plaintiff's attorney or, if the plaintiff does not have an attorney, proof of service upon the plaintiff.

If you have questions, you should see an attorney immediately. If you need help in finding an attorney, you may call the Colorado State Bar's Lawyer Referral Service at (503) 684-3763 or toll-free in Colorado at (800) 452-7636.

                        R. Paul Frasier/OSB # 84223
                        Attorney for Plaintiff

STATE OF COLORADO)
) ss.
COUNTY OF ADAMS   )

IN THE CIRCUIT COURT OF THE STATE OF COLORADO
FOR THE COUNTY OF ADAMS

I, the undersigned attorney of record for the plaintiff, Adams County, certify that the foregoing is an exact and complete copy of the original summons in the above entitled action.

R. Paul Frasier/OSB # 84223
Attorney for Plaintiff

TO THE OFFICER OR OTHER PERSON SERVING THIS SUMMONS:

You are hereby directed to serve a true copy of this summons, together with a true copy of the complaint mentioned herein, upon the individual(s) or other legal entity(ies) to whom which this summons is directed, and to make your proof of service on the following attached page entitled "PROOF OF SERVICE".

R. Paul Frasier/OSB # 84223
Attorney for Plaintiff

IN THE CIRCUIT COURT OF THE STATE OF COLORADO
FOR THE COUNTY OF ADAMS

ADAMS COUNTY, a political
subdivision of the State
of Colorado,

                    Case No. 94CV1067

           Plaintiff,

                    ANSWER

    vs.

REAL PROPERTY LOCATED AT
2755 SHELLEY ROAD, CRIPPLE CREEK,
ADAMS COUNTY, COLORADO,
                Defendant.

      Defendant Teresa M. Patterson by and through her attorney Daniel

M. Hinrichs, appears and answers Plaintiff's complaint filed herein as

follows:

1.

      Defendant admits paragraphs 1 and 2.

2.

      Defendant denies all other allegations contained in Plaintiff's

complaint.

      Dated on this 10th day of January, 1995.

                    DANIEL M. HINRICHS [92591]
                    Attorney for Defendant
                    590 Commercial
                    Adams,, Colorado 97420
                    (503) 267-0229

CERTIFICATE OF MAILING

I certify that I served the foregoing

ANSWER

on the below named persons by depositing a true, full and exact copy thereof in the United States Post Office at Adams,, Colorado, on <u>January 10</u>, 1995, enclosed in a sealed envelope, with postage paid, addressed to:

R. Paul Frasier
District Attorney's Office
Adams County Courthouse
Cripple Creek, Colorado 97423

Attorney for Plaintiff

Daniel M. Hinrichs [92591]
Attorney for Defendant
Teresa M. Patterson

IN THE CIRCUIT COURT OF THE STATE OF COLORADO
FOR THE COUNTY OF ADAMS

ADAMS COUNTY, a political
subdivision of the State
of Colorado,

                                        Case No. 94CV1067

                Plaintiff,

                                        ANSWER

    vs.

REAL PROPERTY LOCATED AT
2755 SHELLEY ROAD, CRIPPLE CREEK,
ADAMS COUNTY, COLORADO,
                Defendant.

Defendant Paul J. Patterson by and through her attorney Michael R.

Lehman, appears and answers Plaintiff's complaint filed herein as

follows:

1.

Defendant admits paragraphs 1 and 2.

2.

Defendant denies all other allegations contained in Plaintiff's

complaint.

Dated on this 9th day of January, 1995.

                        DANIEL M. HINRICHS [92591]
                        Attorney for Defendant
                        590 Commercial
                        Adams,, Colorado 97420
                        (503) 267-0229

ANSWER

I hereby certify that I served a certified copy of the foregoing document on Dan Hinrichs, attorney for the potential claimant, pursuant to ORCP Rule 9 B, C, on November 14th, 1994.

R. Paul Frasier/OSB # 84223
Assistant District Attorney

CERTIFIED TRUE COPY

DISTRICT ATTORNEY'S OFFICE

January 10, 1995

Michael R Lehman
Attorney at Law   Bar #: 78282
590 COMMERCIAL
ADAMS, OR 97420

Adams County/Real Property 2755 Shelley
Case #: 94CV1067

NOTICE OF SCHEDULED COURT PROCEEDING

Scheduled Proceeding: Request Trial Date
Date: 1/25/95
Additional Information:
    MARCH, APRIL,
    MAY, JUNE

The parties must agree upon a trial date under UTCR 7.020. The court prefers the trial date be within the months listed above. The Court must receive three possible agreed upon dates in writing by the above date. Indicated the length of the trial and whether a jury is requested. Jury trials will not be set on Fridays unless four days or more are needed or on Mondays unless five days or more are needed. If the parties cannot agree on a date, they must immediately request a conference with the Presiding Judge.

IF DATES ARE NOT REVEIVED OR A CONFERENCE DOES NOT OCCUR BEFORE THE ABOVE DATE THE COURT WILL SET A ONE DAY TRIAL AT ITS CONVENIENCE.

Client(s) of Addressee:
Paul J. Patterson

CC:
Robert Paul Frasier
Real Property 2755 Shelley Rd.
Teresa M. Patterson

FOR THE CIRCUIT COURT OF THE STATE OF COLORADO
FOR ADAMS COUNTY
250 N. Baxter, Cripple Creek, Colorado 97423
503/396-2121 ext. 259

January 11, 1995

Daniel M Hinrichs
Attorney at Law   Bar #: 92591
590 COMMERCIAL
PO BOX 3605
ADAMS, OR 97420

Adams County/Real Property 2755 Shelley
Case #: 94CV1067

NOTICE OF SCHEDULED COURT PROCEEDING

Scheduled Proceeding: Request Trial Date
Date: 1/25/95
Additional Information:
    MARCH, APRIL,
    MAY, JUNE

    The parties must agree upon a trial date under UTCR 7.020. The
court prefers the trial date be within the months listed above. The Court
must receive three possible agreed upon dates in writing by the above
date. Indicated the length of the trial and whether a jury is requested.
Jury trials will not be set on Fridays unless four days or more are needed
or on Mondays unless five days or more are needed. If the parties
cannot agree on a date, they must immediately request a conference
with the Presiding Judge.
IF DATES ARE NOT REVEIVED OR A CONFERENCE DOES NOT OCCUR
BEFORE THE ABOVE DATE THE COURT WILL SET A ONE DAY TRIAL AT
ITS CONVENIENCE.

Client(s) of Addressee:
Teresa M. Patterson

CC:
Robert Paul Frasier
Real Property 2755 Shelley Rd.
Michael R Lehman

(503) 756-2020 Ext. 576   R. Paul Frasier
FAX   Special Prosecutor
(503) 756-6183   Forfeiture Counsel

January 24, 1994

The Honorable Richard Barron
Presiding Judge
Adams County Circuit Court
Adams County Courthouse
Cripple Creek, Colorado 97423

Re: Adams County v. Real Property located at 2755 Shelley Road,
    Cripple Creek, Colorado. 94-CV-1067

Dear Judge Barron:

        In regards to the trial setting notice that I recently
received, I have spoken with Mr. Dan Hinrichs, attorney for the
claimant Teresa Patterson. Mr. Lehman, attorney for the claimant
Paul Patterson, was unavailable due to his position in the State
Legislature.

        In speaking with Mr. Hinrichs, we would ask that the trial
be set anytime in the week of June 19-23, 1995. I anticipate that
this will be a one day trial.

        If you have any questions, please do not hesitate to
contact me.

        Sincerely,

        R. Paul Frasier

RPF

cc:
Mr. Dan Hinrichs
Mr. Mike Lehman

FOR THE CIRCUIT COURT OF THE STATE OF COLORADO
FOR ADAMS COUNTY
250 N. Baxter, Cripple Creek, Colorado 97423
503/396-2121 ext. 259

January 26, 1995

Robert Paul Frasier
Attorney at Law   Bar #: 84223
SPECIAL NAROTICS PROSECUTOR
1975 MC PHERSON ROOM 302
NORTH BEND OR 97459

Adams County/Real Property 2755 Shelley
Case #: 94CV1067   Civil Forfeiture

NOTICE OF SCHEDULED COURT PROCEEDING

Scheduled Proceeding: Trial Twelve Person Jury
Date: 6/21/95
Time: 9:30AM
Room: Circuit Courtroom, Adams Co. Courthouse,
Cripple Creek

IMPORTANT NOTICE: PLEASE READ

Failure to appear at the court even indicated above at the time and place
specified may result in an order being rendered against you in this case.

Client(s) of Addressee:
Adams County

CC:
Real Property 2755 Shelley Rd
Daniel M Hinrichs
Michael R Lehman

FOR THE CIRCUIT COURT OF THE STATE OF COLORADO
FOR ADAMS COUNTY
250 N. Baxter, Cripple Creek, Colorado 97423
503/396-2121 ext. 259

January 26, 1995

Michael R Lehman
Attorney at Law   Bar #: 78282
590 COMMERCIAL
ADAMS, OR 97420

Adams County/Real Property 2755 Shelley
Case #: 94CV1067   Civil Forfeiture

NOTICE OF SCHEDULED COURT PROCEEDING

Scheduled Proceeding: Trial Twelve Person Jury
Date: 6/21/95
Time: 9:30AM
Room: Circuit Courtroom, Adams Co. Courthouse,
Cripple Creek

IMPORTANT NOTICE: PLEASE READ

Failure to appear at the court even indicated above at the time and place
specified may result in an order being rendered against you in this case.

Client(s) of Addressee:
Paul J. Patterson

CC:
Robert Paul Frasier
Real Property 2755 Shelley Rd
Daniel M Hinrichs

FOR THE CIRCUIT COURT OF THE STATE OF COLORADO
FOR ADAMS COUNTY
250 N. Baxter, Cripple Creek, Colorado 97423
503/396-2121 ext. 259

January 26, 1995

Daniel M Hinrichs
Attorney at Law   Bar #: 92591
590 COMMERCIAL
PO BOX 3605
ADAMS, OR 97420

Adams County/Real Property 2755 Shelley
Case #: 94CV1067   Civil Forfeiture

NOTICE OF SCHEDULED COURT PROCEEDING

Scheduled Proceeding: Trial Twelve Person Jury
Date: 6/21/95
Time: 9:30AM
Room: Circuit Courtroom, Adams Co. Courthouse,
Cripple Creek

IMPORTANT NOTICE: PLEASE READ

Failure to appear at the court even indicated above at the time and place
specified may result in an order being rendered against you in this case.

Client(s) of Addressee:
Teresa M. Patterson

CC:
Robert Paul Frasier
Real Property 2755 Shelley Rd
Michael R Lehman

**IN THE CIRCUIT COURT OF THE STATE OF COLORADO
FOR THE COUNTY OF ADAMS**

ADAMS COUNTY,
          Plaintiff,

vs.

THE REAL PROPERTY LOCATED
AT 2755 SHELLEY ROAD,
CRIPPLE CREEK, ADAMS COUNTY,
COLORADO, ET. AL.,
          Defendants,

Case Number 94CV1067

MOTION AND ORDER

TO DISMISS

COMES NOW the Plaintiff, by and through R. Paul Frasier, Attorney for Plaintiff, and moves this Court to Dismiss the above entitled case without costs to any party or potential claimant on the grounds and for the reason that the issues in the above entitled matter have been fully and completely resolved and satisfied.

Dated this 21st day of April, 1995.

> R. Paul Frasier
> Forfeiture Counsel
> OSB # 84223
> Room # 302
> 1975 McPherson St.
> North Bend, OR 97459
> 756-2020, ext. 559

ORDER

BASED UPON the above motion:

IT IS ORDERED that the above entitled case is dismissed without costs to any party or potential claimant.

Dated this 27th day of April, 1995.

> Richard Barron
> CIRCUIT COURT JUDGE

I hereby certify that I delivered a certified copy of the foregoing document to Mike Lehman, attorney for the potential claimant, pursuant to ORCP Rule 9 B, C, on <u>April 21</u>, 1995.

R. Paul Frasier
SRINT Forfeiture Counsel

IN THE CIRCUIT COURT OF THE STATE OF COLORADO
FOR THE COUNTY OF ADAMS

ADAMS COUNTY,
94CV1067

Case Number

Plaintiff,

vs.

MOTION AND ORDER

TO DISMISS

THE REAL PROPERTY LOCATED
AT 2755 SHELLEY ROAD,
CRIPPLE CREEK, ADAMS COUNTY,
COLORADO, ET. AL.
Defendants,

COMES NOW the Plaintiff, by and through R. Paul Frasier, Attorney for Plaintiff, and moves this Court to Dismiss the above entitled case without costs to any party or potential claimant on the grounds and for the reason that the issues in the above entitled matter have been fully and completely resolved and satisfied.

Dated this 21st day of April, 1995.

R. Paul Frasier
Forfeiture Counsel
OSB # 84223
Room # 302
1975 McPherson St.
North Bend, OR 97459
756-2020, ext. 559

ORDER

BASED UPON the above motion:

IT IS ORDERED that the above entitled case is dismissed without costs to any party or potential claimant.

Dated this 27th day of April, 1995.

_____Richard Barron_____
CIRCUIT COURT JUDGE

Chapter 3

"Sentencing" For Paul & Teresa

FELONY GUIDELINES SENTENCING REPORT
*PLEASE PRESS FIRMLY**   PART A

1 Court Case # 94CR1763	2 Offender's Last Name First MI Patterson Paul J	3 Sex X Male Female	4 Birthdate 09/15/55
5 County of Sentencing Adams	6 Race X White Nat. Am. Asian Black Hispanic Other	7 SID#	8 Date Found Guilty 11/9/94

9 Guilty By
X Plea w/ charge(s) dropped   Stipulated Fact
   Plea to lesser included   Bench Trial
   Plea to original charge(s)   Jury Trial
	10 Supervision Status At Offense
	X None Post-Prison/Parole
	   Probation Incarceration/Escape

11 Did The Case Involve
X No stipulations   Stipulated grid block and presumptive sentence   Stipulated grid block only   Stipulated grid block and departure sentence

12 Most Serious Offense--Primary Manufacture Controlled Substance	13 COS 475.992	14 Seriousness Ranking

15 Offense Modifiers
   Attempt or Solicitation
   Conspiracy
	16
	   Firearm Used
		8

17 Second Most Serious Offense Child Neglect I	18 COS 163.547	19 Seriousness Ranking

20 Offense Modifiers
   Attempt or Solicitation
   Conspiracy
	21
	   Firearm Used
		6

22 Third Most Serious Offense Felon in Possession of Firearm	23 COS 166.270	24 Seriousness Ranking

25 Offense Modifiers
   Attempt or Solicitation
   Conspiracy
	26
	   Firearm Used
		6

27 Supplement attached to report additional current convictions		

28 **CRIMINAL HISTORY CLASSIFICATION   A B C D E F G H I** (CIRCLE)
Record all prior felony and A-misdemeanor convictions on Criminal History Worksheet and attach.

29 The presumptive guideline sentence for the primary offense is:
A prison term of _____ to _____ months and   A probationary sentence A post-prison supervision term of _____ months.   Of _____ months.
30 Additional current convictions: **PRESUMPTIVE RANGE   BASE RANGE** Second most serious _____ to _____ months   _____ to _____ months Third most serious _____ to _____ months   _____ to _____ months

DEPARTMENT OF CORRECTIONS
SANTIAM CORRECTIONAL INSTITUTE
TRANSITIONAL RELEASE SERVICES UNIT
4005 SOUTHEAST AUMSVILLE HIGHWAY
CRIPPLE CREEK, COLORADO 97301 PHONE: 378-5548

ADAMS COUNTY CIRCUIT COURT
HON. JUDGE BARRON
COURTHOUSE
2ND AND BAXTER
CRIPPLE CREEK, COLORADO 97423

Advance Notice—Release of Inmate

On 10/28/96, Paul Patterson DOB: 09/15/55 will become eligible for release programming that may include Transitional Leave.

On 06/02/96, Paul Patterson will become eligible for release programming that may include Work Release or Short-term Emergency Leave.

CASE NUMBER: 94CR1763 DEL/MAN AF

This letter constitutes 30 days notice prior to leave from physical custody pursuant to COS 144.260.

A Parole Release Date of   / /   has been established by the Board of Parole and Post Prison Supervision.

The Sentencing Guidelines Projected Release Date is 11/27/96.

If you would like to know the specific conditions of supervision for this offender, please contact the Board of Parole & Post-Prison Supervision. Phone: 945-0900; FAX 373-7558; 2575 Center Street NE Salem, OR 97310.

DEPARTMENT OF CORRECTIONS
Community Corrections

CONDITIONS OF SUPERVISION

NAME: Paul J. Patterson___
COUNTY: ADAMS_____   Case No. 94CR1763

I. GENERAL CONDITIONS

The Court may place the defendant on probation, which shall be subject to the following General Conditions unless specifically deleted by the Court (COS 137.540). The Probationer shall:

1. Pay supervision fees, fines, restitution or other fees ordered by the Court.

2. Not use or possess controlled substances except pursuant to a medical prescription.

3. Submit to testing of breath or urine for controlled substance or alcohol use if the probationer has a history of substance abuse or if there is a reasonable suspicion that the probationer has illegally used controlled substances

4. Participate in a substance abuse evaluation as directed by the supervising officer and follow the recommendations of the evaluator if there are reasonable grounds to believe there is a history of substance abuse.

5. Remain in the State of Colorado until written permission to leave is granted by the Department of Corrections or a county community corrections agency.

6. If physically able, find and maintain gainful full-time employment, approved schooling, or a full-time combination of both. Any waiver of this requirement must be based on a finding by the Court stating the reasons for the waiver.

7. Change neither employment nor residence without prior permission from the Department of Corrections or a county community corrections agency.

8. Permit the probation officer to visit the probationer or the probationer's residence or work site, and report as required and abide by the direction of the supervising officer.

9. Consent to the search of person, vehicle or premises upon the request of a representative of the supervising officer if the supervising officer

has reasonable ground to believe that evidence of a violation will be found, and submit to fingerprinting or photographing, or both, when requested by the Department of Corrections or a county community corrections agency for supervision purposes.

10. Obey all laws, municipal, county, state and federal.

11. Promptly and truthfully answer all reasonable inquiries by the Department of Corrections or a county community corrections agency.

12. Not possess weapons, firearms or dangerous animals.

13. If under supervision for, or previously convicted of a sex offense under COS 163.305 to 163.465, and if recommended by the supervising officer, successfully complete a sex offender treatment program approved by the supervising officer and submit to polygraph examinations at the direction of the supervising officer.

14. Participate in a mental health evaluation as directed by the supervising officer and follow the recommendation of the evaluator.

II. SPECIAL CONDITIONS

In addition to the General Conditions, the Court may impose any Special Conditions of probation that are reasonably related to the crime of conviction or the needs of the defendant for the protection of the public or reformation of the offender, or both, including, but not limited to, that the Probationer shall:

____1. For crimes committed prior to November 1, 1989, and misdemeanors committed on or after November 1, 1989, be confined to county jail/be restricted to the probationer's own residence or to the premises thereof, or be subject to any combination of such confinement and restriction for a period not to exceed.
_X_2. For felonies committed on or after November 1, 1989, be confined in the county hail or be subject to other custodial sanctions under community supervision, or both, as provided by rules of the State Sentencing Guidelines Board. The Court imposes 180 custody units served at:
____Adams County Jail; ___residential custodial treatment facility
____restitution, probation, work release or community corrections center;
____house arrest; ____community service; ___other: _____
_X_3. Submit to polygraph examination by a qualified polygraph examiner designated by the Court of Probation Officer under terms and conditions set by the Court.
____4A Abstain from the use of intoxicants.
_X_4B Not use intoxicants to excess. (The excessive use of intoxicants is understood to mean that the effects disrupt or interfere with domestic life, employment or proper community conduct.)

____5. Take Antabuse, if medically approved.

____6. Refrain from knowingly associating with persons who use or possess controlled substances illegally, or from frequenting places where such substances are kept or sold.

____7. Refrain from knowingly associating with:

      ____A. Codefendants or crime partners

      ____B. Persons known to be engaged in criminal activities

      ____C. Persons under age ____ except under specific circumstances specified in writing by the Court or Probation Officer.

      ____D. Other designated persons _____

_X_8. Other Special Conditions:

      _X_A. Pay Unitary Assessment of 282.00; pay court-appointed attorney fees of $____; pay fine and court costs of $ 718.00; pay restitution of $_____; FOR TOTAL COURT COSTS OF $608.00, payable at the rate of $100.00 per month beginning 30 days after release from custody through the Adams County Court Administrator's Office

      _X_B. Pay supervision fee as directed by the supervising correctional agency.

Failure

Corrections or a county community corrections agency may result in arrest, modification of conditions, revocation of probation or imposition of structured, intermediate sanctions. The Court may at any time modify the Conditions of Probation.

__11-14-94__	__Richard Barron_____
DATE	JUDGE

I understand and accept the Conditions of Probation under which I have been released by the sentencing Court. I agree to abide by and conform to them and fully understand my failure to do so may result in arrest, modification of conditions, revocation of probation or imposition of structured, intermediate sanctions.

               Paul Patterson_____

DATE   SIGNATURE OF PERSON UNDER SUPERVISION

_____

REVIEWED WITH SUPERVISING OFFICER   DATE

CRIMINAL HISTORY WORKSHEET
(Attach to Felony Guidelines Sentencing Report)

Court Case #   Offenders Last Name   First   MI
94CR1763   Patterson   Paul   J

CONVICTION TYPE

Offense Title	Court and Case #	Date of Conviction	JUVENILE Felony Person NonPer	ADULT Felony Class A Per NonP Per NP
1 Recently stolen Dup	California	10-24-75		X
2 Possession controlled substance	California	8-15-77		X
3 Possession of drugs	California	3-28-78		X
4 Sell & transport marijuana	California	9-19-83		X
5 Possess marijuana for sale	California	11-7-83		X

TOTAL NUMBER OF PRIOR CONVICTIONS BY TYPE:

(Include only those relied
upon in the current proceeding)

PART B

PLEASE PRESS FIRMLY

31 Court Case #   32 Offenders Last Name First MI   33 Sentencing Date
   94CR1763   Patterson Paul J   11-9-94

34 PSI Ordered
   Yes   X No

PROBATION   PRISON

Bench

35. Probation Length: <u>36</u> months X Supervised

              IMPOSITION OF:
              CUSTODY JAIL
              UNITS

36. Most Serious Offense   ____ _90_ days

37. 2nd Most Serious Offense ____ _90_ days

38. 3rd Most Serious Offense ____ _____days

39.   Total   ____ _180_ days

40. Total Financial Conditions $ <u>1,000.00</u>

41. Type of Treatment or Evaluation:
    Drug   Alcohol Mental Health
    Sex Offender Other

43 Most Serious Offense
(Primary): _26_ months
  44 Second Most Serious:
    _____ months
  Concurrent to primary
  sentence
  Consecutive
45 Third Most Serious:
  ___ months
  Concurrent to primary
  sentence
  Consecutive
46 Total Term of Imprisonment
_26_ months
47 This prison term runs:
  Concurrently
  Consecutively
to prior sentence in Case # __
48 Post Prison Supervision:
_36_ months
49 Gun Minimum Imposed:
  Yes
Sentence Pursuant to COS 137.635:
  Yes

FOR OFFENDERS IN 8-G, 8-H OR 8-I

42 Eligible for Optional Probation

Yes
No

If ineligible, cite reason(s):

Treatment not available
Firearm use
Supervision status at offense

50 A departure sentence was
  2nd Most Serious Offense
  3rd Most Serious Offense

51 Type of departure sentence:
  Dispositional
  Durational
  Dispositional and Durational
  Dangerous Offender
  Custody Units

52 FactCOS cited as a basis
      MITIGATING FACTCOS
A. Victim Involvement
B. Defendant Under Duress
C. Defendant's Mental Capactity
D. Offense Accomplished by Another
E. Defendant's Minor Role
F. Defendant's Cooperation w/State
G. Harm or Loss Less than Typical
H. Conviction Free for Significant Period
I.   Other

53 AGGRAVATING FACTCOS

A. Deliberate Cruelty to Victim
B. Victim Particularly Vulnerable
C. Violence Toward Victim or Witness
D. Persistent Similar Offenses
E. Weapon Use
F. Violation of Public Trust
G. Multiple Victims or Incidents
H. Crime Part of Organized Operation
I. Permanent Injury to Person
J. Harm/Loss Greater Than Typical
K. Motivated by Race, Religion, or Sexual Orientation of Victim
L. Other

Sentencing for Teresa Patterson

Ex-City Building Inspector Sentenced On Drug Charge

CRIPPLE CREEK—The former building inspector in Cripple Creek and Gold Mine was sentenced to 32 months in prison after being convicted of growing marijuana at his residence near Cripple Creek.

Three co-defendants with the man, including his wife, have also been convicted in the case.

Paul Jonah Patterson, 39, pleaded no contest to manufacture of the controlled substance marijuana, first-degree child neglect, and being an ex-con in possession of a firearm, said R. Paul Frasier, prosecutor for the South River Interagency Narcotics Team.

Patterson was sentenced to 26 months in prison for the marijuana charge and 90 days each for the child neglect and firearms charges.

Patterson's wife Teresa, 33, pleaded no contest to manufacturing marijuana and first-degree child neglect. She will be sentence Nov. 21, Frasier said.

The Pattersons were arrested on Oct. 12, when police serving a search warrant discovered evidence of a large marijuana growing operation at their residence on Shelley Road near Cripple Creek.

Steven E. Osborn, 37, and Peter A. Oliver, 34, pleaded no contest earlier this month to conspiracy to manufacture marijuana and were each sentenced to 60 days in jail and two years of probation, Frasier said.

F-94-3243-1/CN
    IN THE CIRCUIT COURT OF THE STATE OF COLORADO FOR ADAMS
COUNTY

THE STATE OF COLORADO,
                Plaintiff,

                                                    INDICTMENT

        vs.
                                                    Case No. 94CR2156

Teresa Patterson,
                Defendant.

                09/31/61*

Teresa Patterson is accused by the Grand Jury for the County of Adams, State of
Colorado, by this indictment of the crime(s) of

COUNT 1: SUPPLYING CONTRABAND, COS 162.185, Class CF

COMMITTED AS FOLLOWS:
                                COUNT 1:
The said defendant, on or about the 21st day of December, 1994, in Adams
County, Colorado, did unlawfully and knowingly introduce tobacco, contraband,
into the Adams County Jail, a correctional facility; contrary to the statutes in such
cases made and provided and against the peace and dignity of the State of
Colorado.

The District Attorney opposes violation treatment of all misdemeanors alleged in
this Indictment.

Witnesses examined before the Grand Jury:
Lee Embree

Dated: __12-27__, 1994 at Cripple Creek, Adams County, Colorado.

                                ____Peter Blyth_____
                                District Attorney

                                _____Is_____ A TRUE BILL

                                ____Arlene Johnson_____
                                Foreperson of the Grand Jury

**IN THE DISTRICT COURT IN THE STATE OF COLORADO
FOR THE COUNTY OF ADAMS**

THE STATE OF COLORADO,
                    Plaintiff,

            vs.   Case No. 94CR1756 PV
Teresa M. Patterson____   94CR2156 Supplying Contraband
            Defendant

_____
            True Name

The following proceedings were held in the above-captioned case before the
undersigned judge on ___12-28-94___.

_____Paul Frasier_____ District Attorney appearing for the State.

(X) Arraignment /New Charge/Continued/DA Info/Detainer/Fugitive Complaint
( ) Plea
( ) Arraignment-Probation Violation/Contempt/RO Violation/Diversion Violation
( ) Defendant failed to appear. B/W ordered, Security Bail set $ _____
( ) Other: _____

(X) Defendant appeared with counsel ____Nick Nylander_____
( ) Defendant appeared without counsel, was informed right to retained or
appointed counsel and the court appointed _____/continued proceedings
to _____ so defendant could retain counsel.
( ) Defendant waived right to counsel.

(X) Defendant advised of right to jury trial/hearing and confrontation, privilege
against self-incrimination, and all other procedures and penalties required by law.

( ) Counsel for defendant waived reading of accusatory instrument, acknowledged
receipt of a certified true copy.
(X) The Court delivered a certified true copy to the defendant

( ) Defendant waived Identity Hearing/Writ of Habeas Corpus/Extradition and
signed a waiver and the court ordered defendant to be held _____ days.

( ) Defendant ordered to report to jail forthwith to be booked and released.
( ) Defendant entered a plea of ( ) Not Guilty ( ) Guilty ( ) Divert ( ) No Contest
    ( ) Admitted Probation Violation to the following charges: _____
_____

( ) Other: _____
( ) Pay $ _____ By _____ and balance at $ _____ Month beginning _____ or
                                            appear at 9AM next Judicial day.
(X) THE ABOVE CASE HAS BEEN GIVEN A DAY AND TIME CERTAIN FOR:
PV/Omni/Identity/Preliminary/Extradition/RO _____ at _____
Writ of Habeas Corpus/Contempt of Court: _____ at _____
Plea: 1/6/95 at 9:00 AM. Sentencing: _____ at _____
Trial: _____ at

_____
PSI: ( ) Requested ( ) Waived ( ) Further Time Waived
Other: _____
Cancel date of _____

_____ Dismissed Pursuant to Plea bargain.
The following arrangements were made for the release of the defendant:
( ) Release on own recognizance   ( ) Security set at $ _____
( ) Defendant held in custody   ( ) Bail set at $ _____

Dated <u>12-28-94</u>   Reporter <u>Kay Marino</u>   ___<u>Richard Barron</u>_____
                                                                 District/Circuit Judge

IN THE CIRCUIT COURT OF THE STATE OF COLORADO
FOR THE COUNTY OF ADAMS

STATE OF COLORADO
     v.   Case No. 94CR1756
Teresa M. Patterson   _____
Defendant   _____

                      (X) Judgment of Conviction/Sentence
                      ( ) Order on Probation Violation/Sentence

The above named Defendant coming before this court on 11-21-94, the State appearing by Paul Frasier, Assistant District Attorney; Defendant appearing in person and by attorney Dan Hinrichs; Defendant being advised of the right to counsel and pled NO CONTEST to and is convicted of the following offenses.

Case/Count	Offense
2	MFG CS- marijuana
7	CHILD NEGLECT I

IT IS HEREBY ORDERED:
1.____ DRUG DIVERSION- Defendant's guilty plea to PCS _____ is accepted
       under COS 475.245
   ____ an adjudication of guilt ( ) shall not be ( ) is entered at this time
2._X_ Counts dismissed: __Remaining Charges_____
   ___Cases dismissed: _____
3.____ Presentence report ( ) received ( ) waived
4.____ DEFENDANT IS SENTENCE TO:
   ____ _____ days/months Adams County Jail
   ____ _____ months/years Department of Corrections; followed by _____
      months post-prison supervision
   ____ pay fines, costs, fees, assessments, restitution as set forth in the Money
      Judgment section below
   ____ _____ months Dangerous Offender _____ months gun minimum
   ____ early release for residential drug/alcohol treatment
5._X_ PROBATION:
  _X_ (X) sentenced to probation for ___48___ months _____ to the:
     _X_ Department of Corrections (see attached sheet for conditions)
     ____ Court (see attached sheet for conditions)
  ____ Court finds jail space available and imposes: _____ sanction units
    effective ( ) immediately ( ) beginning on _____, at _____ AM/PM
  ____ early release for drug/alcohol residential treatment
  ____ _____ hours community service to be completed by _____
  ____ comply with previously imposed conditions of probation
  _X_ serve 150 days in the Adams County jail effective (X) immediately ( )
    beginning on _____, at _____ AM/PM.
6.____ OTHER ORDERS: __ NO CREDIT- (90 days on Ct. 7 and 60 days on Ct. 2-
_____ consecutively to each other) _____

MONEY JUDGMENT   Case/Count   Amount
    _94CR1756_

    _____   _____

Judgment Creditor: State of Colorado   Total Judgment Amount $ _1,000.00_

Judgment Debtor: Teresa Patterson   SSN _____

UNAS $ _188.00_   FINE $ _753.00_   OPTS $ _____   REST $ _____   COMP $ _____

ATFE $ _____   DICO $ _____   COST $ _____   CJAS $ _54.00_   LEML $ _5.00_

Restitution:

    Name and Address   Amount

1._____
    _____ $_____
    _____

2._____
    _____ $_____
    _____

3._____
    _____ $_____
    _____

4._____
    _____ $_____
    _____

PAYMENT TERMS:

____ Immediately due
_X_ at $ _25.00_ per month, beginning _30 days after release from custody._
____ bail or security is applied
____ restitution joint and several with _____ in Case No. _____
____ report to court at 9:00 AM the next judicial day if your payment is not made
in full as ordered.
____ to be set by court collections officer
____ other: _____

Payable To:

STATE COURT ACCOUNTING, ADAMS COUNTY COURTHOUSE
CRIPPLE CREEK, OR 97423

Dated this _23rd_ day of _November_, 19 _94._

Reporter: __Kay Marino_____   ____Richard Barron_____
                                        Circuit/District Judge
Interpreter: _____

DEPARTMENT OF CORRECTIONS
Community Supervision

CONDITIONS OF SUPERVISION

NAME: Teresa Patterson
County: ADAMS_____   Case # 94CR2156

I.GENERAL CONDITIONS:
The court may place the defendant on probation, which shall be subject to the following General Conditions unless specifically deleted by the Court (COS 137.540). The Probationer shall:

1. Pay supervision fees, fines, restitution or other fees ordered by the Court.
2. Not use or possess controlled substances except pursuant to a medical prescription.
3. Submit to testing of breath or urine for controlled substance or alcohol use if the probationer has a history of substance abuse or if there is a reasonable suspicion that the probationer has illegally used controlled substances.
4. Participate in a substance abuse evaluation as directed by the supervising officer and follow the recommendations of the evaluator if there are reasonable grounds to believe there is a history of substance abuse.
5. Remain in the State of Colorado until written permission to leave is granted by the Department of Corrections or a county community corrections agency.
6. If physically able, find and maintain gainful full-time employment, approved schooling, or a full-time combination of both. Any waiver of this requirement must be based on a finding by the Court stating the reasons for the waiver.
7. Change neither employment nor residence without prior permission from the Department of Corrections or a county community corrections agency.
8. Permit the probation officer to visit the probationer or the probationer's residence or work site, and report as required and abide by the direction of the supervising officer.
9. Consent to the search of person, vehicle or premises upon the request of a representative of the supervising officer if the supervising officer has reasonable grounds to believe that evidence of a violation will be found, and submit to fingerprinting or photographing, or both, when requested by the Department of Corrections or a county community corrections agency for supervision purposes.
10. Obey all laws, municipal, county, state and federal.
11. Promptly and truthfully answer all reasonable inquiries by the Department of Corrections or a county community corrections agency.
12. Not possess weapons, firearms or dangerous animals
13. If under supervision for, or previously convicted of a sex offense under COS 163.305 to 163.465, and if recommended by the supervising officer, successfully complete a sex offender treatment program approved by the supervising officer and submit to polygraph examinations at the direction of the supervising officer.
14. Participate in a mental health evaluation as directed by the supervising officer and follow the recommendation of the evaluator.

SPECIAL CONDITIONS:
In addition to the general conditions, the Court may impose any special conditions of probation that are reasonably related to the crime of conviction or the needs of the defendant for the protection of the public or reformation of the offender, or both, including, but not limited to, that the Probationer shall:

___ 1. For crimes committed prior to November 1, 1989, and misdemeanors committed on or after November 1, 1989, be confined to the county jail/be restricted to the probationer's own residence or to the premises thereof, or be subject to any combination of such confinement and restriction for a period not to exceed _____

_X_ 2. For felonies committed on or after November 1, 1989, be confined in the county jail or be subject to other custodial sanctions under community supervision, or both, as provided by the rules of the State Sentencing Guidelines Board. The Court imposes 60 custody units served at:
   _x_ jail; ___ residential custodial treatment facility;
   ___ restitution, probation, work release or community service center;
   ___ house arrest; ___ community service; ___ other: _____

___ 3. Submit to polygraph examination by a qualified polygraph examiner designated by the Court or Probation Officer under terms and conditions set by the Court.

___ 4A Abstain from the use of intoxicants.

___ 4B Not use intoxicants to excess. (The excessive use of intoxicants is understood to mean that the effects disrupt or interfere with domestic life employment or proper community conduct.)

___ 5. Take Antabuse, if medically approved.

___ 6. Refrain from knowingly associating with persons who use of possess controlled substances illegally, or from requesting places where such substances are kept or sold.

___ 7. Refrain from knowingly associating with:
   ___ A. Codefendants or crime partners.
   ___ B. Persons known to be engaged in criminal activities.
   ___ C. Persons under age ___ except under specific circumstances specified in writing by the Court or Probation Officer.
   ___ D. Other designated persons _____

_X_ 8. Other Special Conditions:
   _x_ A. Pay Unitary Assessment of $ 54.00, pay court appointed attorney fees of $ _____, fay fine and costs of $ _____, for total court costs of $ _____, payable at the rate of $ 10.00 per month beginning *_____ through the Adams County Court Administrator's Office.
   _x_ B. Pay supervision fee as directed by the supervising correctional agency.
   _x_ C. Come until condition in 94CR1766*

Failure to abide by all general and special conditions imposed by the Court and supervised by the Department of Corrections or a county community corrections agency may result in arrest, modification of conditions, revocation or probation or imposition of structured, intermediate sanctions. The Court may at any time modify the Conditions of Probation.

_1-6-95_   __Richard Barron_____
DATE   JUDGE

I understand and accept the Conditions of Probation under which I have been released by the sentencing Court. I agree to abide by and conform to the and fully understand my failure to do so may result in arrest, modification of conditions, revocation of probation or imposition of structured, intermediate sanctions. No * o no doops*

_____   _____Teresa Patterson_____
DATE   SIGNATURE OF PERSON UNDER SUPERVISION

_____   _____
REVIEWED WITH SUPERVISING OFFICER   DATE

IN THE CIRCUIT COURT OF THE STATE OF COLORADO
FOR ADAMS COUNTY

STATE OF COLORADO,
          PLAINTIFF,   No. 94CR2156
                          94CR1766

    vs.

                           PLAINTIFF'S DESIGNATION OF
TERESA M. PATTERSON,   ATTORNEY
          DEFENDANT

        Notice is hereby given that the attorney of record for the State on this matter will be:

                  R. Paul Frasier
                  S.R.I.N.T.
                  South River Interagency Narcotics Team
                  1975 McPherson, Room # 302
                  Denver, Colorado 97459

                  Telephone: (503) 756-2020 ext. 576
                  FAX: (503) 756-6183

        Any communications regarding this matter are requested to be sent to the above attorney at the above address or phone number.

        Dated this 28th day of December, 1994.

                  R. Paul Frasier OSB # 84223
                  Special Narcotics Prosecutor

****

I certify that I served a true copy of this document on Nick Nylander, attorney for the defendant, in compliance with the applicable rules of the Colorado Rules of Civil Procedure on the 28th of December, 1994.

                  R. Paul Frasier OSB # 84223
                  Special Narcotics Prosecutor

PART B

PLEASE PRESS FIRMLY

31 Court Case #	32 Offenders Last Name	First	MI	33 Sentencing Date
94CR2156	Patterson	Teresa	M	1-6-95

34 PSI Ordered
Yes X No

PROBATION   ## PRISON

Bench

35. Probation Length: <u>24 </u>months   X Supervised

IMPOSITION OF:
CUSTODY JAIL
UNITS

36. Most Serious Offense   ___ _60_ days

37. 2nd Most Serious Offense ___ ___ days

38. 3rd Most Serious Offense ___ ___days

39.   Total   ___ _60_ days

40. Total Financial Conditions $ 94.00

41. Type of Treatment or Evaluation:
Drug   Alcohol   Mental Health
Sex Offender   Other

43 Most Serious Offense
(Primary): ____ months
44 Second Most Serious:
_____ months
Concurrent to primary
sentence
Consecutive
45 Third Most Serious:
___ months
Concurrent to primary
sentence
Consecutive
46 Total Term of Imprisonment
___ months
47 This prison term runs:
Concurrently
Consecutively
to prior sentence in Case # __
48 Post Prison Supervision:
____ months
49 Gun Minimum Imposed:
Yes
Sentence Pursuant to COS 137.635:
Yes

FOR OFFENDERS IN 8-G, 8-H OR 8-I

42 Eligible for Optional Probation   Yes
                                                 No

If ineligible, cite reason(s):   Treatment not available
                                     Firearm use
                                     Supervision status at offense

50 A departure sentence was
    2nd Most Serious Offense
    3rd Most Serious Offense

51 Type of departure sentence:
    Dispositional
    Durational
    Dispositional and Durational
    Dangerous Offender
    Custody Units

52 FactCOS cited as a basis
           MITIGATING FACTCOS
A. Victim Involvement
B. Defendant Under Duress
C. Defendant's Mental Capacity
D. Offense Accomplished by Another
E. Defendant's Minor Role
F. Defendant's Cooperation w/State
G. Harm or Loss Less than Typical
H. Conviction Free for Significant Period
I. Other

53 AGGRAVATING FACTCOS

    A. Deliberate Cruelty to Victim
    B. Victim Particularly Vulnerable
    C. Violence Toward Victim or Witness
    D. Persistent Similar Offenses
    E. Weapon Use
    F. Violation of Public Trust
    G. Multiple Victims or Incidents
    H. Crime Part of Organized Operation
    I. Permanent Injury to Person
    J. Harm/Loss Greater Than Typical
    K. Motivated by Race, Religion, or Sexual Orientation of Victim
    L. Other

FELONY GUIDELINES SENTENCING REPORT

*PLEASE PRESS FIRMLY   **PART A**

1 Court Case # 94CR2156	2 Offender's Last Name First MI Patterson Teresa M	3 Sex Male X Female	4 Birthdate 09-31-61
5 County of Sentencing ADAMS	6 Race X White Nat. Am. Asian Black Hispanic Other	7 SID #	8 Date Found Guilty 1-6-95

9 Guilty By
  Plea w/ charge(s) dropped Stipulated Fact
  Plea to lesser included   Bench Trial
X Plea to original charge(s) Jury Trial
	10 Supervision Status At Offense
	  None Post-Prison/Parole
	X Probation Incarceration/Escape

11 Did The Case Involve	
No Stipulations	Stipulated grid block and presumptive sentencing
Stipulated grid block only	Stipulated grid block and departure sentence

12 Most Serious Offense Supplying Contraband	13 COS 162.185	14 Seriousness Ranking **4**

15 Offense Modifiers
  Attempt or Solicitation
  Conspiracy
	16 Firearm Used	

17 Second Most Serious Offense	18 COS	19 Seriousness Ranking

20 Offense Modifiers
  Attempt or Solicitation
  Conspiracy
	21 Firearm Used	

22 Third Most Serious Offense	23 COS	24 Seriousness Ranking

25 Offense Modifiers
  Attempt or Solicitation
  Conspiracy
	26 Firearm Used	

27 Supplement attached to report additional current convictions

28 CRIMINAL HISTORY CLASSIFICATION A B C D E F G H I
  (CIRCLE)

Record all prior felony and A-misdemeanor convictions on Criminal History Worksheet and attach.

---

29 The presumptive guideline sentence for the primary offense is:
A prison term of _____ to_____ months and   X A probationary sentence   a post-prison supervision term of _____ months.   of _24_ months

30 Additional current convictions: **PRESUMPTIVE RANGE**   **BASE RANGE**
Second most serious _____ to _____ months   _____ to _____ months   Third most serious _____ to _____ months   _____ to _____ months

IN THE CIRCUIT COURT OF THE STATE OF COLORADO
FOR THE COUNTY OF ADAMS

STATE OF COLORADO
          Plaintiff,   Case No. 94CR2156

vs.   PETITION TO ENTER PLEA OF GUILTY
                                      AND ORDER ENTERING PLEA

Teresa M. Patterson
          Defendant.

1. My full true name is <u>Teresa Matthews Patterson</u>, and I am (X) am not ( ) an American citizen. I understand that if I am not an American citizen I can be deported from the United States, excluded from admission to the United States, or denied naturalization as an American citizen.

2. I am represented by a lawyer whose name is <u>Nick Nylander.</u>

3. I have received a copy of the accusatory instrument filed against me.

4. I wish to plead guilty to the charge(s) of: <u>Supplying Contraband</u>

    ____ (a) Class A. Felony:
    ____ (b) Felony seriously endangering life/safety of another:
    ____ (c) Other crimes: _____

5. I know if I plead guilty to the charges, the maximum possible sentence is _5_ years imprisonment and/or a fine of $ 100,000.00. I know also that the sentence is up to the court only.

6. I have (X) have not ( ) been convicted of one or more felonies in the past as follows: ___ Child Neglect I & Manufacturing a controlled substance___

7. I also know if I am pleading guilty to a felony that seriously endangered the life/safety of another and I have a prior felony conviction or I am pleading guilty to a class A felony, it may be decided I am a dangerous offender and the maximum sentence may be increased to 30 years for each such charge.

8. I am (X) am not ( ) presently on probation or parole. I understand that by pleading guilty in this case my probation or parole may be revoked. I further understand that if my parole or probation is revoked, any sentence in that case may be consecutive to or in addition to any sentence in this case.

9. I understand that by pleading guilty I give up my right to have a jury trial and agree that a judge alone can decide my case. I know a jury has 12 citizens of Adams County on it and it takes 10 out of 12 to find me guilty or not guilty.

10. I understand that by pleading guilty I give up my right to confront the witnesses against me. I know this means that I do not get to see, hear and question the witnesses against me in court. I know that no witnesses are necessary because I am pleading guilty.

11. I understand that by pleading guilty I give up my privilege against self-incrimination. I know this means I will have to admit committing a crime whereas if I pleaded not guilty, I could remain totally silent and not say

anything about the charges against me and my silence would not be used against me.

12. I know that by pleading guilty it will not be necessary for the state to prove my guilt beyond a reasonable doubt and I also know that by pleading guilty I will no longer be presumed to be not guilty of the crimes with which I am charged.

13. I understand that by pleading guilty I can only appeal to a higher court about the sentence the judge gives me. I know that this means that I lose my right to complain to a higher court about errors, if any, made by the police, the prosecution, my attorney or the judge.

14. I OFFER MY PLEA OF "GUILTY" FREELY AND VOLUNTARILY AND OF MY OWN ACCORD AND WITH FULL UNDERSTANDING OF ALL THE MATTERS SET FORTH IN THE INDICTMENT ( ) INFORMATION ( ) AND THIS PETITION.

15. I request the court to enter my plea of "Guilty".

SIGNED by me in open court this 6th day of January, 19 95.

_____Teresa Patterson_____
Defendant

Witness: _____Nick Nylander_____
        Attorney for Defendant

ORDER

IT IS ORDERED that the defendant's plea of "GUILTY" be accepted and entered as prayed for in the petition.

Done in open court this 6th day of January, 19 95.

_____Richard Barron_____
Circuit Court Judge

CRIMINAL HISTORY WORKSHEET

(Attach to a Felony Guidelines Sentencing Report)

Court Case #
94CR2156

Offender's Last Name   First   MI
Patterson   Teresa   M

CONVICTION TYPE

Offense Title	Court and Case #	Date of Conviction	Juvenile Felony Per Nonper	Adult Felony Per Nonper	Adult Class-A Per Nonper
1 Child Neglect I	Adams 94CR1766	11-9-94		X	
2 MCS-MI	Adams 94CR1766	11-9-94		X	

TOTAL NUMBER OF PRIOR CONVICTIONS BY TYPE:

(Include only those relied upon in the current proceeding)

IN THE CIRCUIT COURT FOR THE STATE OF COLORADO
FOR THE COUNTY OF ADAMS

THE STATE OF COLORADO,
                              Plaintiff,
    vs.

Teresa Patterson
    Defendant

_____
    True Name

**RECORD OF PROCEEDINGS
AND ORDER**

Case No. 94CR1756 PV
94CR2156 Supplying Contraband

The following proceedings were held in the above-captioned case before the undersigned judge on 1-6-95__

_____Paul Frasier_____District Attorney appearing for the State

( ) Arraignment/New Charge/Continued/DA Info/Detainer/Fugitive Complaint
(X) Plea
( ) Arraignment-Probation Violation/Contempt/RO Violation/Diversion Violation
( ) Defendant failed to appear. B/W ordered, Security/Bail set $ _____
( ) Other: _____

( ) Defendant appeared with counsel _____Nick Nylander_____
( ) Defendant appeared without counsel, was informed of right to retained or
    appointed counsel and the court appointed _____/continued
    proceedings to _____ so defendant could retain counsel.
( ) Defendant waived right to counsel

( ) Defendant advised of right to jury trial/hearing and confrontation, privilege
    against self-incrimination, and all other procedures and penalties required by
    law.

( ) Counsel for defendant waived reading of accusatory instrument, acknowledged
    receipt of a certified true copy.
( ) The Court ( ) district attorney, read the indictment/information/fugitive
    complaint to the defendant/delivered a certified true copy to the defendant.

( ) Defendant waived Identity Hearing/Writ of Habeas Corpus/Extradition and
    signed a waiver and the court ordered defendant to be held _____ days.

( ) Defendant ordered to report to jail forthwith to be booked and released
( ) Defendant entered a plea of ( ) Not Guilty (X) Guilty ( ) Divert ( ) No Contest
    ( ) Admitted Probation Violation to the following charges: ___94CR2156_____
_____

( ) Other: State will not revoke probation on 94CR1766
( ) Pay $ _____ By _____ and balance at $ _____/Month beginning _____
                    or appear at 9AM the next judicial day

(X) THE ABOVE CASE HAS BEEN GIVEN A DAY AND TIME CERTAIN FOR:
    PV/Omni/Identity/Preliminary/Extradition/RO _____ at _____
    Writ of Habeas Corpus/Contempt of Court: _____ at _____
    Plea: _____ at _____. Sentencing: __Today_____ at _____
    Trial: _____ at _____
    PSI: ( ) Requested ( ) Waived ( ) Further Time Waived

Other: _____

( ) Cancel date of _____

( ) _____ Dismissed Pursuant to Plea bargain.

The following arrangements were made for the release of the defendant:

( ) Release on own recognizance.　　( ) Security set at $ _____

( ) Defendant held in custody.　　( ) Bail set at $ _____

Dated __1-6-95__　　Reporter __Kay Marino__　　___Richard Barron____

　　　　　　　　　　　　　　　　　　　　　　　District/Circuit Judge

cc: Jail, DA, Def, Atty, P&P

IN THE CIRCUIT/DISTRICT COURT OF THE STATE OF COLORADO
FOR THE COUNTY OF ADAMS

STATE OF COLORADO   Case No. <u>94CR2156</u>

      v.   _____

<u>Teresa Patterson</u>

Defendant.   _____

                      (X) Judgment of Conviction/Sentence
                      ( ) Order on Probation Violation/Sentence

The above named Defendant coming before this court on <u>1-6-95</u>, the State appearing by <u>Paul Frasier</u>, Assistant District Attorney; Defendant appearing in person and by attorney <u>Nick Nylander</u>; Defendant being advised of the right of counsel and pled <u>GUILTY</u> to and is convicted of the following offenses:

Case/Count	Offense
_____	<u> SUPPLYING CONTRABAND </u>
_____	_____
_____	_____

IT IS HEREBY ORDERED:

1.____ DRUG DIVERSION- Defendant's guilty plea to PCS _____ is accepted
        under COS 475.245
    ____ an adjudication of guilt ( ) shall not be ( ) is entered at this time
2.____ Counts dismissed: __Remaining Charges_____
   ____Cases dismissed: _____
3.____ Presentence report ( ) received ( ) waived
4.____ DEFENDANT IS SENTENCE TO:
    ____ _____ days/months Adams County Jail
    ____ _____ months/years Department of Corrections; followed by _____
        months post-prison supervision
    ____ pay fines, costs, fees, assessments, restitution as set forth in the Money
        Judgment section below
    ____ _____ months Dangerous Offender _____ months gun minimum
    ____ early release for residential drug/alcohol treatment
5._X_ PROBATION:
  _X_ (X) sentenced to probation for __24___ months _____ to the:
      _X_ Department of Corrections (see attached sheet for conditions)
      ____ Court (see attached sheet for conditions)
  _X_ Court finds jail space available and imposes: __60__ sanction units
     effective (X) immediately consecutively to time now serving.
  ____ early release for drug/alcohol residential treatment
  ____ _____ hours community service to be completed by _____
  _X_ comply with previously imposed conditions of probation
  ____ serve ___ days in the Adams County jail effective ( ) immediately ( )
     beginning on _____, at _____ AM/PM.
6.____ OTHER ORDERS: _____
_____

IN THE CIRCUIT COURT FOR THE STATE OF COLORADO
FOR ADAMS COUNTY

STATE OF COLORADO

       Plaintiff,

       vs.

Paul Jonah Patterson and
Teresa M. Patterson
       Defendants

Case No. 94CR1756
       94CR1763
       94CR2156

SATISFACTION OF MONEY
JUDGMENT

STATE OF COLORADO

County of Adams

       Plaintiff acknowledges satisfaction of the amounts stated in the Money Judgments made and docketed in the above-entitled court and cause.

       Dated on April 26th, 1995.

       PAUL R. BURGETT
       District Attorney for Adams County
       Adams County Courthouse
       Cripple Creek, OR 97423

       By: _____Paul R. Burgett_____

Subscribed and sworn to before me on ____April 26th, 1995____.

       _____Laurie K. Kreutzer_____
       NOTARY PUBLIC FOR COLORADO

       My commission Expires: _10-14-97_.

CERTIFICATE OF SERVICE BY MAIL

       I certify that on April 26th, 1995, I served the foregoing Satisfaction of Money Judgment upon the defendants hereto by mailing, regular mail, postage prepaid, a true, exact and full copy thereof to:

       Ticor Title Company
       P.O. Box 368
       Cripple Creek, Colorado 97423

       R. Paul Frasier
       District Attorney/Assistant
       Adams County Courthouse
       Cripple Creek, OR 97423

MONEY JUDGMENT

Case/Count
__94CR2156__

Amount
_____
_____
_____

Judgment Creditor: State of Colorado   Total Judgment Amount $ _95.00__

Judgment Debtor: _Teresa M. Patterson_   SSN _____

UNAS $ 94.00   FINE $_____   OPTS $ _____   REST $ _____   COMP $ _____

ATFE $ _____   DICO $ _____   COST $ _____   CJAS $ _____   LEML $ _____

Restitution:

Name and Address	Amount
1._____	$ _____
_____	
_____	
2._____	$ _____
_____	
_____	
3._____	$ _____
_____	
_____	

PAYMENT TERMS:
____ Immediately due
_X_ at $ _10.00_ per month, beginning _30 days after release from custody_
____ bail or security is applied
____ restitution joint and several with _____
____ report to court at 9:00 AM the next judicial day if your payment is not made
in full as ordered.
____ to be set by court collections officer
____ other: _____

Payable To:

**STATE COURT ACCOUNTING, ADAMS COUNTY COURTHOUSE
CRIPPLE CREEK, OR 97423**

Dated this _17_th day of _January_, 19 _95._

Reporter: __Kay Marino_____   ____Richard Barron_____
                                                    Circuit/District Judge
Interpreter: _____

IN THE CIRCUIT/DISTRICT COURT OF THE STATE OF COLORADO FOR ADAMS COUNTY

STATE OF COLORADO,

        Plaintiff,

vs.

Teresa Patterson

        Defendant.

Case No: 94CR1756

MOTION TO REVOKE
PROBATION

The District Attorney's Office for Adams County, Colorado herby moves the Court for an Order that the Defendant's probation herein be revoked on the ground(s) set out in the <u>Special Information Report</u> of the Parole and Probation Department dated May 4, 1995, which is annexed hereto and by this reference incorporated herein.

        Dated: May 5, 1995.

                PAUL R. BURGETT
                District Attorney for Adams County
                By: Paul R. Burgett
                District Attorney/Assistant

ORDER

IT IS HEREBY ORDERED that:

        Said Defendant be brought before the above-entitled Court at the earliest opportunity to show cause, if any there be, why probation heretofore granted should not be revoked and sentence imposed.

        Dated at Cripple Creek, Colorado, on   <u>5-5-95</u> .

                <u>Richard Barron</u>
                CIRCUIT COURT JUDGE

COLORADO DEPARTMENT OF CORRECTIONS Date   SID NUMBER
   ADULT PAROLE AND PROBATION   5-4-95_____

DETENTION WARRANT

NAME OF VIOLATOR
____Patterson, Teresa_____

TO: ANY SHERIFF OF PEACE OFFICER OF THE
STATE OF COLORADO

PLACE OF CONFINEMENT
_____CCJ_____

This will serve as your authority to hold the
person named as a

AUTHORITY HELD FOR
____COS. 144.350_____

X Probation Violator
  Parole Violator
  Interstate Compact Violator
  Institution Leave Violator

Pending Disposition by:

X Court
  Parole Board
  Department of Corrections

HONORABLE _____R L Barron_____
The person named is being detained by
this department for your disposition as an
alleged violator. A full report covering alleged
violation will be promptly submitted.

Bond May Not Be Posted
While Warrant Is In Force

FRANK A. HALL, Director
Department of Corrections

By:

__Terri L. Hatenpiller_____
ADULT PAROLE AND PROBATION OFFICER

____Adams___ County   Docket No. 94CR1766

Alleged Violations:

      Gen. Cond. # 10: "Obey all laws..." by committing the new crime
      of Filing False Police Report.

      Gen. Cond. # 11: "Answer Truthfully..." by lying to Po about
      diamond ring.

COLORADO DEPARTMENT OF CORRECTIONS
Adams County Community Corrections
Adams County Branch Office
155 North Adams, Suite B, Cripple Creek, OR 97423
(503) 396-3173; 269-0714

SPECIAL INFORMATION REPORT—NOTICE OF VIOLATION

NAME: PATTERSON, TERESA M. _____ DATE: MAY 4, 1995
ADDRESS: 2755 SHELLEY ROAD, CRIPPLE CREEK, OR 97423
CASE TYPE: FELONY PROBATION   SID #: _____
CRIME: DEL/MAN AF; CHILD NEG I; SUPP CONT
SENTENCE: 48 MOS; 48 MOS; 24 MOS_____ AGE/DOB: 33 (9/31/61)
COUNTY/DOCKET#: ADAMS/94CR1766; 94CR1756; 94CR2156
JUDGE: RICHARD L. BARRON_____
EXPIRATION DATE: 11/20/98; 11/20/98; 1/05/97

REPORT SUBMITTED BY: TERI HATZENPILLER, ADULT PAROLE & PROBATION
OFFICER
REPORT APPROVED BY: STEVE LIDAY, DIRECTOR, ADAMS COUNTY COMM. CORR.

PRESENTING PROBLEM—VIOLATED GENERAL CONDITIONS #10 & #11
(COMMITTED NEW CRIME OF FILING FALSE POLICE REPORT & LYING TO PO
ABOUT DIAMOND RING:

On 04/26/95, Lt. Ogden called writer saying he was in receipt of a letter
from subject accusing Adams County Corrections of keeping her diamond ring
(approximate value $1,400-3,000), when her property was returned on 03/08/95.
Writer called subject asking her about this letter. She claimed the same story with
writer. Writer told her if the situation was true, then she should file a report with
the Cripple Creek Police Department. Writer instructed her that she would be
taking a polygraph subsequent to filing the report and if the polygraph came our
deceptive, she may be looking at new criminal charges. She acknowledged that
she understood the process. Subject filed the complaint with Cripple Creek Police
on 04/27/95. Writer telephoned subject in the afternoon of 04/27/95 and directed
her to report for polygraph on 05/02/95 at 8:30 a.m. On 05/02/95, Don Ross,
probation officer and polygraph examiner, returned from administering the
polygraph to subject, saying subject was deceptive on all questions regarding the
ring and subject maintained throughout with the examiner that her story was
true. Subject reported to the DOC office as directed following the polygraph.
Subject insisted she was telling the truth. Writer asked Director Steve Liday if he
would return to writer's office and speak to subject. Subject admitted to Mr. Liday
that she "lied" and did the act because she was "pissed off at the system." Mr.
Liday requested that subject write and admission statement which she did. After
Mr. Liday left the room, writer asked subject why she did not tell the truth earlier
in the meeting and she said, through tears, "I was praying the polygraph would
come up truthful." Cripple Creek Police Officer Ray Nichols formally charged
subject with filing a false report on 05/04/95. He then arrested and transported
subject to the Adams County Jail.

RECOMMENDATION:
____ NO ACTION AT THIS TIME; INFORMATION ONLY.
_X_ INVESTIGATION CONTINUING; FORMAL REPORT TO FOLLOW.
____ OTHER (INDICATED BELOW):

NOTICE OF VIOLATION/FELONY PROBATION

SPECIAL CONDITIONS:

CASE NO. 94CR1756

On 11/21/94, Patterson was placed on 48 months' probation to the Colorado Department of Corrections, subject to all General Conditions. The Court imposed 120 custody units each on Counts II and VII with 90 units ordered served in the Adams County Jail on Count II and 60 on Count VII, consecutively to each other. The Court also ordered the following Special Conditions: (3) Polygraph; (4B) No intoxicants to excess; (6) No association with drug users or places; (8A) Pay Unitary Assessment of $188 and fine of $812; total court costs $1,000 payable at the rate of $25 per month beginning 30 days after release from custody; (8B) Pay supervision fees.

On 11/21/94, the original sentence order was amended to change the custody units ordered served to 60 units on each count consecutively to each other.

CASE NO. 94CR2156

On 01/06/95, Patterson was placed on 24 months' probation to the Colorado Department of Corrections, subject to all General Conditions. The Court imposed 120 custody units with 60 ordered served in the Adams County Jail consecutive to time being served and no credit. The Court also ordered the following Special Conditions: (8A) Pay Unitary Assessment of $94 payable at the rate of $10 per month beginning 30 days after release from custody; (8B) Pay supervision fees.

ALLEGATIONS:

1.   Patterson violated General Condition #10: "Obey all laws, municipal, county, state, and federal," by committing the new crime of Initiating a False Report.

2.   Patterson violated General Condition #11: "Promptly and truthfully answer all reasonable inquiries by the Department of Corrections or a county community corrections agency," by lying to her probation officer about the circumstances surrounding her diamond ring.

SUBSTANTIATION OF ALLEGATIONS:

1.& 2.
On 04/24/95, Lt. Gordon Ogden of the Adams County Jail called writer to say he was in receipt of a letter from Teresa Patterson which said in substance that the Adams County Jail had not returned her half-carat, diamond solitare ring, which she said was placed in her property during booking on 11/21/94. Subsequent to her release on 03/08/95, subject says in a letter that she went to two local jewelers and got

NOTICE OF VIOLATION/FELONY PROBATION

estimates of replacement (ranging from $1,400 to $3,000). Patterson states clearly in her letter that she expected the ring to be returned to her, or be reimbursed at replacement value. Since this was a very serious allegation, writer called subject at home and asked her about the letter. She maintained that all was true and that she has a sales receipt for the ring, which she used to get the estimates. Writer then said if what she said was true, she should go immediately to the Cripple Creek Police Department and file a police report. Writer cautioned her about filing a false report, telling her that after she filed, she would be scheduled for a polygraph examination, and if the polygraph results proved deceptive, she may be looking at new charges. Again, she repeated she was telling the truth and that she would be going to the Cripple Creek Police Department at 8:00 a.m. the next morning to file her complaint. Writer directed subject to report to the Department of Corrections' office after she made her report. Subject reported as directed and provided a copy of the letter that she wrote to Lt. Ogden and a copy of a receipt for the ring in question.

After consulting polygraph examiner Don Ross, writer called subject in the afternoon of 04/25/95, directing her to report to the Department of Corrections' office on 05/02/95 at 8:25 a.m. for polygraph examination with instructions to report to writer directly following the exam.

On 05/02/95, polygraph examiner Don Ross returned from the polygraph examination of subject saying that subject's response to the three relevant questions regarding the ring came up consistently indicative of deception, and she kept repeating she was telling the truth to examiner Ross. With this information, writer brought subject into her office and confronted subject with the results, asking her to clear the air with the truth of the situation. Through tears and dramatics, she continued to maintain she was telling the truth.

Writer then went to Director Steve Liday to staff the situation, in the end requesting Mr. Liday to return to subject's interview with writer. Mr. Liday started by calmly requesting that subject quiet herself. Initially, she maintained her story with Mr. Liday, but at one point Mr. Liday used the analogy of subject "digging a hole for herself" with the story, pointing out that the end result had only two conclusions. The truth would begin the process of unburying herself; the other was to dig the hole deeper until she was totally buried. Shortly thereafter, subject said she lied about the whole thing. To Mr. Liday's question, "Why did you do it?" she responded she was "pissed off at the system." Mr. Liday then requested she write out an admission statement, which she did. It was agreed that subject would return to the Department of Corrections' office on 05/04/95 at 1:30 p.m. to give time to consider the next appropriate action. At the conclusion of the interview, writer asked subject why she did not tell the truth earlier, and again through tears, she stated that she was praying that the polygraph would come up truthful.

NOTICE OF VIOLATION/FELONY PROBATION

On 05/04/95, subject reported to the Department of Corrections' office at 1:30 p.m. Cripple Creek Police Officer Ray Nichols was present in writer's office and interviewed subject regarding all of the above, after giving Patterson her Miranda rights. Officer Nichols showed subject the handwritten admission statement and asked if she wrote it, to which she said yes. He then asked her if she knew that she was filing a false police report, to which she said yes. Officer Nichols then arrested subject with writer performing the patdown search. Writer asked subject to remove all her jewelry and to place it in her purse. Subject first requested writer to give the purse to her boyfriend, Patrick (PJ) Johnson, then requested she watch writer hand over the purse to Johnson. Although an unusual courtesy in an arrest situation, under the circumstances it felt prudent that writer grant the request. Thereafter Officer Nichols transported subject to the Adams County Jail.

CONFORMANCE/EVALUATION:

Subject report to the Department of Corrections' office upon her release from the original and subsequent Supplying Contraband sentence on 03/10/95. In less than two months of community supervision, she is once again being returned to Court on the new crime of Initiating a False Report and not truthfully answering her probation officer's questions. It appears that Patterson is her own worst enemy in terms of personal accountability. From the beginning of this supervision, Ms. Patterson has minimized her responsibility for her unlawful behaviors and has remained resistant to any notion that her own conduct placed her in the criminal justice system. Patterson has paid off all her court costs from the proceeds of the sale of her 10-acre property on Shelley Road.

RECOMMENDATION:

It is, therefore, respectfully recommended that Teresa Matthews Patterson be returned to Court to show cause why her probation should not be revoked. If found in violation, it is further recommended that probation be continued under all previously-imposed conditions and the following additional Special Condition:

2. Be confined to the Adams County Jail to serve all unused custody units (254 units) in Case Nos. 94CR1766 and 94CR2156.

___5/10/95___	___Steve Liday_____
DATE	(FOR) TERRI HATZENPILLER
	Adult Parole & Probation Officer

___5/10/95___	___Steve Liday_____
DATE	STEVE LIDAY, Director
	Adams County Community

Corrections

STATE OF COLORADO
DEPARTMENT OF CORRECTIONS
ADAMS COUNTY COMMUNITY CORRECTIONS

CUSTODY STATUS: IN CUSTODY ADAMS COUNTY JAIL; DETAINER FILED 05/04/95

PURPOSE OF REPORT: NOTICE OF VIOLATION/FELONY PROBATION

DATE: MAY 10, 1995

PROBATION OFFICER: TERI HATZENPILLER, ADULT PAROLE & PROBATION OFFICER, ADAMS BRANCH OFFICE, 155 NORTH ADAMS, SUITE B, CRIPPLE CREEK, OR 97423 (396-3173, EXT. 240) CASELOAD #6204

NAME: PATTERSON, TERESA MATTHEWS

ADDRESS: 2755 SHELLEY ROAD, CRIPPLE CREEK, OR 97423

SID: DOB: 33 (DOB: 09/31/61)

CRIME: COUNT II, CASE NO. 94CR1766: DEL/MAN AF—MARIJUANA
        COUNT VII, CASE NO. 94CR1766: CHILD NEGLECT I
        CASE NO. 94CR2156: SUPPLYING CONTRABAND

SENTENCE: CASE NO. 94CR1763: 48 MONTHS' PROBATION
          CASE NO. 94CR2156: 24 MONTHS' PROBATION

COUNTY: ADAMS   DOCKET#: 94CR1763; 94CR2156

JUDGE: RICHARD L. BARRON

EXPIRATION DATE: CASE NO. 94CR1756: 11/20/98; CASE NO. 94CR2156: 01/05/97

COMPACT___ LEAVE___ PAROLE___ PROBATION _X_ POST-PRISON___

SUPERVISION LEVEL: HIGH   RISK ASSESSMENT SCORE: 7

CUSTODY UNITS:

COUNT II, CASE NO. 94CR1756:   COUNT VII, CASE NO. 94CR1756:

CUSTODY UNITS IMPOSED: 120   CUSTODY UNITS IMPOSED: 120
CUSTODY UNITS SERVED: 32   CUSTODY UNITS SERVED: 32
CUSTODY UNITS AVAILABLE: 88   CUSTODY UNITS AVAILABLE: 88

CASE NO. 94CR2156, SUPP. CONT:

CUSTODY UNITS IMPOSED: 120
CUSTODY UNITS SERVED: 42
CUSTODY UNITS AVAILABLE: 78

IN THE CIRCUIT/DISTRICT COURT OF THE STATE OF COLORADO
FOR ADAMS COUNTY

STATE OF COLORADO.

        Plaintiff,

vs.

Teresa Patterson,

        Defendant.

Case No. 94CR2156

A M E N D E D
MOTION TO REVOKE
PROBATION

The District Attorney's Office for Adams County, Colorado hereby moves the Court for an Order that the Defendant's probation herein be revoked on the ground(s) set out in the ALLEGATIONS section of the Parole and Probation Department report dated May 10, 1995 which is annexed hereto and by this reference incorporated herein.

Nick Nylander, attorney at law, represents Defendant and has waived formal presentment of this Motion. Pursuant to this stipulation, I hereby certify that I have mailed true and accurate copy of the above-named Motion to said attorney.

Dated: May 11, 1995.

PAUL R. BURGETT
District Attorney for Adams County

By: ___Christopher W. Owens_
District Attorney/Assistant

ORDER

IT IS HEREBY ORDERED that:

Said Defendant be brought before the above-entitled Court and show cause, if any there be, why probation heretofore granted should not be revoked and sentence imposed.

Probation Revocation Hearing: May 12, 1995.

Dated at Cripple Creek, Colorado on ___05-12-95___.

___Richard Barron_____
CIRCUIT COURT JUDGE

DEPARTMENT OF CORRECTIONS
Community Corrections
CONDITIONS OF SUPERVISION

NAME: TERESA PATTERSON
COUNTY: ADAMS_____   Case No. 94CR1756 & 94CR2156

I.GENERAL CONDTIONS:

The Court may place the defendant of probation, which shall be subject to the following General Conditions unless specifically deleted by the Court (COS 137.540). The Probationer shall:

1. Pay supervision fees, fines, restitution or other fees ordered by the Court.
2. Not use or possess controlled substances except pursuant to a medical prescription.
3. Submit to testing of breath or urine for controlled substance or alcohol use if the probationer has a history of substance abuse or if there is a reasonable suspicion that the probationer has illegally used controlled substances.
4. Participate in a substance abuse evaluation as directed by the supervising officer and follow the recommendations of the evaluator if there are reasonable grounds to believe there is a history of substance abuse.
5. Remain in the state of COLORADO until written permission to leave is granted by the Department of Corrections or a county community corrections agency.
6. If physically able, find and maintain gainful full-time employment, approved schooling, or a full-time combination of both. Any waiver on this requirement must be based on a finding by the Court stating the reasons for the waiver.
7. Change neither employment nor residence without prior permission from the Department of Corrections or a county community corrections agency.
8. Permit the probation officer to visit the probationer or the probationer's residence or work site, and report as required to abide by the direction of the supervising officer.
9. Consent to the search of person, vehicle or premises upon the request of a representative of the supervising officer if the supervising officer has reasonable grounds to believe that the evidence of a violation will be found, and submit to fingerprinting or photographing, or both, when requested by the Department of Corrections or a county community corrections agency for supervision purpose.
10. Obey all laws, municipal, county, state and federal.
11. Promptly and truthfully answer all reasonable inquiries by the Department of Corrections or a county community corrections agency.
12. Not possess weapons, firearms or dangerous animals.
13. If under supervision, or previously convicted of a sex offense under COS 163.305 to 163.465, and if recommended by the supervising officer, successfully complete a sex offender treatment program approved by the supervising officer and submit to polygraph examinations at the direction of the supervising officer.
14. Participate in a mental health evaluation as directed by the supervising officer and follow the recommendation of the evaluator.

II. SPECIAL CONDITIONS:

In addition to the General Conditions, the Court may impose any Special Conditions of probation that are reasonably related to the crime of conviction or the needs of the defendant for the protection of the public or reformation of the offender, or both, including, but not limited to, that the Probationer shall:

_____1. For crimes committed prior to November 1, 1989, and misdemeanors committed on or after November 1, 1989, be confined to the county jail/be restricted to the probationer's own residence or to the premises thereof, or be subject to any combination of such confinement and restriction for a period not to exceed _____ days.

_____2. For felonies committed on or after November 1, 1989, be confined in the county jail or be subject to other custodial sanctions under community supervision, or both, as provided by rules of the State Sentencing Guidelines Board. The Court imposes <u>254</u> custody units served at:
    <u>X</u> Adams County Jail; ____ residential custodial treatment facility
    ____ restitution, probation, work release or community corrections center
    ____ house arrest; ____ community service; __ other_____

_____3. Submit to polygraph examination by a qualified polygraph examiner designated by the Court or Probation Officer under terms and conditions set by the Court.

_____4A Abstain from the use of intoxicants

_____4B Not use intoxicants to excess. (The excessive use of intoxicants is understood to mean that the effects disrupt or interfere with domestic life, employment or proper community conduct.

_____5. Take Antabuse, if medically approved.

_____6. Refrain from knowingly associating with persons who use or possess controlled substances illegally, or from frequenting places where such substances are kept or sold.

_____7. Refrain from knowingly associating with:
    ____A. Codefendants or crime partners.
    ____B. Persons known to be engaged in criminal activities.
    ____C. Persons under age ____ except under specific circumstances specified in writing by the Court or Probation Officer.
    ____D. Other designated persons _____

<u>X</u>_8. Other Special Conditions:
    <u>X</u>_A. Pay Unitary Assessment of $_____; pay court-appointed attorney fees of $_____; pay fine and court costs of $_____; pay restitution of $_____; FOR TOTAL COURT COSTS OF $_____, payable at the rate of $_____ per month beginning _____ through the Adams County Court Administrator's Office.
    <u>X</u>_B. Pay supervision fee as directed by the supervising correctional agency.

Failure to abide by all General and Special Conditions imposed by the Court and supervised by the Department of Corrections or a county community corrections agency may result in arrest, modification or conditions, revocation of probation or imposition of structured, intermediate sanctions. The Court may at any time modify the Conditions of Probation.

__05-12-95__	____Richard Barron_____
DATE	JUDGE

I understand and accept the Conditions or Probation under which I have been released by the Sentencing Court. I agree to abide by and conform to them and fully understand my failure to do so may result in arrest, modification of conditions, revocation of probation or imposition of structured, intermediate sanctions.

May 12, 1995   Teresa Patterson
DATE   SIGNATURE OF PERSON UNDER SUPERVISION

John Brown
REVIEWED WITH SUPERVISING OFFICER   DATE

DEPARTMENT OF CORRECTIONS
Community Corrections
CONDITIONS OF SUPERVISION

NAME: <u>TERESA PATTERSON</u>
COUNTY: <u>ADAMS</u>   Case No. 94CR1756 & 94CR2156

I.GENERAL CONDTIONS:

The Court may place the defendant of probation, which shall be subject to the following General Conditions unless specifically deleted by the Court (COS 137.540). The Probationer shall:

1. Pay supervision fees, fines, restitution or other fees ordered by the Court.
2. Not use or possess controlled substances except pursuant to a medical prescription.
3. Submit to testing of breath or urine for controlled substance or alcohol use if the probationer has a history of substance abuse or if there is a reasonable suspicion that the probationer has illegally used controlled substances.
4. Participate in a substance abuse evaluation as directed by the supervising officer and follow the recommendations of the evaluator if there are reasonable grounds to believe there is a history of substance abuse.
5. Remain in the state of COLORADO until written permission to leave is granted by the Department of Corrections or a county community corrections agency.
6. If physically able, find and maintain gainful full-time employment, approved schooling, or a full-time combination of both. Any waiver on this requirement must be based on a finding by the Court stating the reasons for the waiver.
7. Change neither employment nor residence without prior permission from the Department of Corrections or a county community corrections agency.
8. Permit the probation officer to visit the probationer or the probationer's residence or work site, and report as required to abide by the direction of the supervising officer.
9. Consent to the search of person, vehicle or premises upon the request of a representative of the supervising officer if the supervising officer has reasonable grounds to believe that the evidence of a violation will be found, and submit to fingerprinting or photographing, or both, when requested by the Department of Corrections or a county community corrections agency for supervision purpose.
10. Obey all laws, municipal, county, state and federal.
11. Promptly and truthfully answer all reasonable inquiries by the Department of Corrections or a county community corrections agency.
12. Not possess weapons, firearms or dangerous animals.
13. If under supervision, or previously convicted of a sex offense under COS 163.305 to 163.465, and if recommended by the supervising officer, successfully complete a sex offender treatment program approved by the supervising officer and submit to polygraph examinations at the direction of the supervising officer.
14. Participate in a mental health evaluation as directed by the supervising officer and follow the recommendation of the evaluator.

II.SPECIAL CONDITIONS:

In addition to the General Conditions, the Court may impose any Special Conditions of probation that are reasonably related to the crime of conviction or the needs of the defendant for the protection of the public or reformation of the offender, or both, including, but not limited to, that the Probationer shall:

____1. For crimes committed prior to November 1, 1989, and misdemeanors committed on or after November 1, 1989, be confined to the county jail/be restricted to the probationer's own residence or to the premises thereof, or be subject to any combination of such confinement and restriction for a period not to exceed _____ days.

_X_2. For felonies committed on or after November 1, 1989, be confined in the county jail or be subject to other custodial sanctions under community supervision, or both, as provided by rules of the State Sentencing Guidelines Board. The Court imposes 254 custody units served at:
   _X_ Adams County Jail; ____ residential custodial treatment facility
   ____ restitution, probation, work release or community corrections center
   ____ house arrest; ____ community service; ___ other_____

_X_3. Submit to polygraph examination by a qualified polygraph examiner designated by the Court or Probation Officer under terms and conditions set by the Court.

____4A Abstain from the use of intoxicants

_X_4B Not use intoxicants to excess. (The excessive use of intoxicants is understood to mean that the effects disrupt or interfere with domestic life, employment or proper community conduct.

____5. Take Antabuse, if medically approved.

_X_6. Refrain from knowingly associating with persons who use or possess controlled substances illegally, or from frequenting places where such substances are kept or sold.

____7. Refrain from knowingly associating with:
   ____A. Codefendants or crime partners.
   ____B. Persons known to be engaged in criminal activities.
   ____C. Persons under age ____ except under specific circumstances specified in writing by the Court or Probation Officer.
   ____D. Other designated persons _____

_X_8. Other Special Conditions:
   _X_A. Pay Unitary Assessment of $282.00; pay court-appointed attorney fees of $___0___; pay fine and court costs of $ 812.00 ; pay restitution of $_0_; FOR TOTAL COURT COSTS OF $ 1,094.00, payable at the rate of $ 25.00 per month beginning 30 days after release from custody through the Adams County Court Administrator's Office (PAID IN FULL).
   _X_B. Pay supervision fee as directed by the supervising correctional agency.

Failure to abide by all General and Special Conditions imposed by the Court and supervised by the Department of Corrections or a county community corrections agency may result in arrest, modification or conditions, revocation of probation or imposition of structured, intermediate sanctions. The Court may at any time modify the Conditions of Probation.

_____	__Richard Barron_____
DATE	JUDGE

I understand and accept the Conditions or Probation under which I have been released by the Sentencing Court. I agree to abide by and conform to them and fully understand my failure to do so may result in arrest, modification of conditions, revocation of probation or imposition of structured, intermediate sanctions.

_____	_____Teresa Patterson_____
DATE	SIGNATURE OF PERSON UNDER SUPERVISION

____John Brown_____

REVIEWED WITH SUPERVISING OFFICER   DATE

MONEY JUDGMENT

Case/Count   Amount

_____   _____

_____   _____

_____   _____

Judgment Creditor: State of Colorado   Total Judgment Amount $

_____

Judgment Debtor: _____   SSN _____

UNAS $ _____ FINE $ _____ OPTS $ _____ REST $ _____ COMP $_____

ATFE $ _____ DICO $ _____ COST $_____ CJAS $ _____ LEML $_____

Restitution:

Name and Address   Amount

1._____ $_____

_____

_____

2._____ $_____

_____

_____

3._____ $_____

_____

_____

PAYMENT TERMS:

___ Immediately due
___ at $_____ per month, beginning _____
___ bail or security is applied
___ restitution joint and several with _____ in Case No. _____
___ report to court at 9:00 AM the next judicial day if your payment is not made
    in full as ordered.
___ to be set by court collections officer
___ other: _____

Payable To:

STATE COURT ACCOUNTING, ADAMS COUNTY COURTHOUSE,CRIPPLE CREEK, OR
97423

Dated this 18th day of May, 19 95.

                    __R. Paul Frasier_____
                    Circuit/District Judge

Reporter: __Kay Marino__

Interpreter: __Rebecca Berg__

IN THE DISTRICT COURT IN THE STATE OF COLORADO
FOR THE COUNTY OF ADAMS

THE STATE OF COLORADO,   **RECORD OF**
PROCEEDINGS

                              Plaintiff,   **AND ORDER**

              vs.

                                                 Case No. 94CR1756 PV
Teresa Patterson   94CR2156 Supplying Contraband
        Defendant

_____
        True Name

The following proceedings were held in the above-captioned case before the
undersigned judge on 5-12-95___

___Chris Owen_____ District Attorney appearing for the State

( ) Arraignment/New Charge/Continued/DA Info/Detainer/Fugitive Complaint
(X) Plea
( ) Arraignment-Probation Violation/Contempt/RO Violation/Diversion Violation
( ) Defendant failed to appear. B/W ordered, Security/Bail set $ _____
( ) Other: _____

(X) Defendant appeared with counsel _____Nick Nylander_____
( ) Defendant appeared without counsel, was informed of right to retained or
     appointed counsel and the court appointed _____/continued
     proceedings to _____ so defendant could retain counsel.
( ) Defendant waived right to counsel

( ) Defendant advised of right to jury trial/hearing and confrontation, privilege
     against self-incrimination, and all other procedures and penalties required by
     law.

( ) Counsel for defendant waived reading of accusatory instrument, acknowledged
     receipt of a certified true copy.
( ) The Court ( ) district attorney, read the indictment/information/fugitive
     complaint to the defendant/delivered a certified true copy to the defendant.

( ) Defendant waived Identity Hearing/Writ of Habeas Corpus/Extradition and
     signed a waiver and the court ordered defendant to be held _____ days.

(X) Defendant ordered to report to jail forthwith to be booked and released
(X) Defendant entered a plea of ( ) Not Guilty ( ) Guilty ( ) Divert ( ) No Contest
     (X) Admitted Probation Violation to the following charges: ___94CR2156_____
     _____
( ) Other: _____
( ) Pay $ _____ By _____ and balance at $ _____/Month beginning _____
                                       or appear at 9AM the next judicial day

(X) THE ABOVE CASE HAS BEEN GIVEN A DAY AND TIME CERTAIN FOR:
     PV/Omni/Identity/Preliminary/Extradition/RO _____ at _____
     Writ of Habeas Corpus/Contempt of Court: _____ at _____
     Plea: _____ at _____. Sentencing: __Today_____ at _____
     Trial: _____ at _____

PSI: ( ) Requested ( ) Waived ( ) Further Time Waived
   Other: _____
( ) Cancel date of _____
( ) _____ Dismissed Pursuant to Plea bargain.

The following arrangements were made for the release of the defendant:
( ) Release on own recognizance.   ( ) Security set at $ _____
( ) Defendant held in custody.   ( ) Bail set at $ _____

Dated __5-12-95__   Reporter _____   __Richard Barron_____
                                                       District/Circuit Judge

cc: Jail, DA, Def, Atty, P&P

IN THE CIRCUIT/DISTRICT COURT OF THE STATE OF COLORADO
FOR THE COUNTY OF ADAMS

STATE OF COLORADO   Case No. 94CR1756
       v.   94CR2156
Teresa Patterson   _____
Defendant.

       ( ) Judgment of Conviction/Sentence
       (X) Order on Probation Violation/Sentence

The above named Defendant coming before this court on 5-12-95, the State appearing by Chris Owen, Assistant District Attorney; Defendant appearing in person and by attorney Nick Nylander; Defendant being advised of the right of counsel and admitted to being in violation of probation of the following offenses:

Case/Count	Offense
94CR1756	(2) MFG. CS—Marijuana (7) CHILD NEGLECT I
94CR2156	SUPPLYING CONTRABAND
_____	_____

IT IS HEREBY ORDERED:
1.____ DRUG DIVERSION- Defendant's guilty plea to PCS _____ is accepted under COS 475.245
     ____ an adjudication of guilt ( ) shall not be ( ) is entered at this time
2.____ Counts dismissed: __Remaining Charges_____
    ___Cases dismissed: _____
3.____ Presentence report ( ) received ( ) waived
4.____ DEFENDANT IS SENTENCED TO:
     ____ _____ days/months Adams County Jail
     ____ _____ months/years Department of Corrections; followed by _____ months post-prison supervision
     ____ pay fines, costs, fees, assessments, restitution as set forth in the Money Judgment section below
     ____ _____ months Dangerous Offender _____ months gun minimum
     ____ early release for residential drug/alcohol treatment
5._X_ PROBATION: ON BOTH CASES
    _X_ (X) sentenced to probation for __3_ years from today's date to the:
         _X_ Department of Corrections (see attached sheet for conditions)
         ____ Court (see attached sheet for conditions)
    _X_ Court finds jail space available and imposes: _254_ sanction units effective (X) immediately. NO CREDIT FOR TIME SERVED.
     ____ early release for drug/alcohol residential treatment
     ____ _____ hours community service to be completed by _____
    _X_ comply with previously imposed conditions of probation
     ____ serve ____ days in the Adams County jail effective ( ) immediately ( ) beginning on _____, at _____ AM/PM.
6.____ OTHER ORDERS: _____
_____

Colorado

April 12, 1996

DIANE CANNON, CIRCUIT COURT CLERK
ADAMS COUNTY COURTHOUSE
CRIPPLE CREEK, OR 97423

DEAR DIANE,

Just to let you know, Teresa Patterson Adams County Case **94CR1756, 94CR2156** has been transferred to INTERSTATE COMPACT DIVISION—2575 CENTER ST NE, SALEM; Phone: 945-9066. Offender gives her new address as 3530 Maryland Circle, Cleveland, TN 37311.

BYE FOR NOW,
Becky Leiper,
Office Specialist I

BL
C—File
  --Court Accounting
  --CSW Director
  --GR

Chapter 4

Prison Life

You, my reader, be the judge.

Honestly, I don't remember all or many details of what occurred over twenty years ago. One thing I do know is what happened did happen, that's for sure.

One thing I know for certain is what occurred in 1996 changed my life forever. This is an account of the events that took place in 1996.

The day was March 6, 1996. Even though the winter had been a hard one and spring was just in the distance, it seemed everyone was ready for spring to start! In Eastern Colorado, it seemed spring was always late compared to Denver weather.

The weather felt crisp that morning as I got out of my car. I was struck by the American flag, the stars and stripes unfurled, a symbol of freedom while the razor wire could be seen covering the perimeter of the prison compound. With the razor wire in place, there was no way an inmate could get out without endangering his life. Only once did an inmate succeed in getting over the high razor wire. That was ten years ago and he was captured, his skin ripped to shreds.

I walked through the gate after pushing a button. A correctional officer identified me and made the appropriate action that would allow me to enter the inner circle of the prison. I was now inside the prison compound. The next step would be to show my picture identification. This procedure would allow the C.O. to give me my keys. The keys opened my office and several other areas of the alcohol and drug treatment program. The C.O. threw the keys under a glass opening in his officer's station. After exchanging the usual "good morning", I then headed a short distance to my office. Before I reached the A&D unit, I saw Officer Harris. Officer Harris said I would be receiving a new inmate today. Wednesdays were the usual day for inmate transfers from the labor side to A&D, although they sometimes occurred on Mondays, too.

Officer Harris appeared to be in a good mood with a big smile on his face as he greeted me.

After informing me that I would get a new client, Officer Harris added, "The inmate is a real hard nut to crack." His name was Paul Patterson. He had been on the labor side for about two months.

I remember Officer Harris made the comment when I was promoted to Counselor IV.

"Are you sure you want to be a Counselor IV,? Every Counselor IV has been terminated in the history of the A&D Program." My response was to laugh it off. I had never been fired while on a job and had worked since I was 11 years old. Although it made the job more challenging to have a difficult client, it was all the more rewarding to see a client make progress and change his life around. The change wouldn't take place overnight. Inmates were usually in the alcohol and drug treatment program for six months on average.

I have worked for the agency since 1989, starting out as a Counselor Trainee in a Detox Unit of Adams House. Adams House was an Inpatient Alcohol and Drug Treatment Program. Usually clients stayed 90 days. Before they could start the 90 day program, clients had to go through detox. While an employee of Adams House, Cripple Creek Correctional Facility was opened in 1989. CCCF was a minimum security prison with a population of roughly 100 inmates, 50 if which were housed in the Alcohol and Drug Treatment Program by Adams House. Staff was contracted by the State of Colorado and considered contracted employees. To sum it up, contracted employees didn't receive the same salary or benefits as state employees.

Today, I went directly to my office. Elaine, who I shared an office with, was already at her desk, work in hand. Elaine was a motherly and nurturing person. She often wore her feelings on her sleeve, which made her a very valued counselor and we enjoyed each other's company.

Elaine left the office to do her 8:30 therapy group as usual. I started doing paperwork, which included progress notes, reviewing a database on a new client named Paul Patterson, and preparing for my weekly criminality class. I can remember distinctly Paul entering my office, as the door was open. He said I needed to watch this video he was watching. People were "Running To the Lord" in Pensacola, Florida. Paul really wanted me to watch the video. As I recollect, I left my office and entered the Assessment Room, still standing at the entrance. The video was in color and in fact people were running to the Lord. The video left quite an impression on me. Paul was very thoughtful and wanted me to see the video. A client had never been so forthcoming in my nearly six years at CCAD.

Although I couldn't stay to watch the video, I asked Joe Bush, the prison minister, if I could borrow the video to watch at home that evening. He gave me the video and encouraged me to watch it.

Years later, in 2016, I ran into Joe Bush as he was entering the local Rite-Aid story. I, of course, said hi to him and once again asked if I could watch the video "Running to the Lord" again. He gave me his card and said to give him a call. I asked if he remembered Paul Patterson. He said he did remember Paul. I told him I would be seeing Paul in March.

Joe said, "Tell him hi."

Joe Bush ministered to Paul while he was at CCAD. To this day, he is a minister and conducts a service of First Street in Adams City. His wife is a loving woman and assists him in his work as a minister. Joe still works for prison fellowship. This is a valuable group that assists inmates in their path to recovery and starting a new life outside prison walls. Joe is a dedicated follower of the Lord and a disciple of Jesus.

I thanked Paul for including me to watch the video during our next one-on-one counseling session. During that one-on-one, I assigned to Paul his autobiography of his life. This would tell his story of the years he was growing up in Berkeley and Oakland, California. The autobiography could also shed some light on his relationship with his parents. Both parents were still alive. Paul was an only child. From his database, which was sixteen pages long and included his criminal history, I discovered he was born in Minneapolis, Minnesota. He was forty years old. His wife's name was Teresa. Teresa and he had been married for fourteen years. He also had a girlfriend named Cherie. She wanted to marry him very badly. Once I entered his room, which he shared with three other inmates. Paul had a photograph of Cherie. It was one of those glamour shots or photos that were popular in the 70s and 80s. She was blonde and attractive. A feathered boa was draped across her shoulders.

One thing I wanted to talk with Pau about was the crime he committed in 1994. He appeared to be resistant to discussing the crime. Looking back at those one-on-ones, I think he felt guilty for putting his children through the pain of going into protective custody and the whole aftermath of his actions in 1994, dating back to his arrest on December 12, 1994.

During those first one-on-ones, Paul appeared depressed, certainly withdrawn. He was beginning to come to terms with taking responsibility for his actions. A major goal at CCAD was for an inmate to take responsibility for their crimes and their actions. As counselors, we taught responsibility and accountability. The program confronted their criminality as we as their alcoholism and drug addiction. The criminality portion confronted their thinking process which included 40 thinking errors, which they used while committing a crime and secondly, they wore criminal masks while in their daily life, such as the "good guy" and "nice guy" mask used in conjunction with their thinking errors. I taught criminality and confronted their thinking while in the class and during one-on-ones. A third part to their Criminality was the use of obstruction tactics to obstruct the change agent; in this case, it was the staff and counselors who were attempting to bring about change in the inmate. Power and control was the viewpoint that the inmate held on to in order to maintain their stance with everyone that they encountered in their daily life.

I taught Criminality for 3 years and it was particularly helpful to get into the workings and psychology of the inmate. Most clients were resistive when they entered CCAD. It is like peeling an onion to get to the root of their criminality and alcoholism and drug addiction.

Paul was resisting, but seemed more open to discussing his issues than other clients that I had while a counselor at CCAD. He was the "hard nut to crack" as Correctional Officer Ken had told me in March of 1996. One thing was for sure: he didn't like that I had so much authority over him. He was his own person and very independent in thought and action.

Throughout the months, I observed the change in Paul and even myself. It was a process of discovery and growth and change. We had a relationship. He was my client and I was his counselor, but, more than that, we were friends. I am talking about sharing and caring. Talking about feelings and emotions. Talking about good and bad times in our lives. Talking about the past, present, and future. Listening to each other's ideas, hopes, and dreams. Sharing what hobbies we liked to do in our spare time, such as photography, fly fishing, decorating, and golfing. We mirrored each other and had natural interests even though we were two very independent people.

Our relationship was a simple one. As a counselor at CCAD, I was attempting to bring about change and was the change agent. Paul was an inmate and client at CCAD who was resisting the change agent and change process.

The six months that Paul was at CCAD went fast. Looking back, I recall one day when Paul was in the day area. He was talking to a fellow inmate about weird things that were happening. I overheard their conversation.

My response was to go up to Paul by saying, "They aren't weird, they are just meant to be!" Walking away, I don't know what happened after that. There were other times in which I felt I knew or had met Paul somewhere before in time. It was a déjà vu moment.

Remembering a time while teaching criminality, I called on Paul to answer a question. I called out his name, Paul. He told me later, during a one-on-one, it was as if he heard his name called out during a previous time long ago by me. It was as if I had met Paul during a previous lifetime and that he had met me, too. This premonition haunts me to this day.

There were other days at CCAD that were a little bit crazy. These were busy days. Between lots of paperwork, the day was a constant go, go, go.

I recall one day that had been a little more hectic than normal.

Turning to Paul as he was coming out of his room, I said, "This day has been really crazy and I think I will join a nunnery!" Although the comment was meant to be a joke, the comment describes how right I was feeling on that day. Paul smiled at me as he walked away, headed to take a shower.

At CCAD, we had daily interchanges where, as staff, we discussed the day and particular, our clients. In addition, the four counselor IVs met with John Carey, our supervisor. When you saw John Carey, he towered over you like a tall building. He was over seven feet tall. Had had a nickname, "Big John." He often mentioned his size when talking to you. He carried his size with him. For myself, his size intimidated me. His size commanded and spoke of authority. When he talked, your immediate response was to listen to him and not interrupt him.

There were weekly meetings during which Counselor IVs met with him. One time when we met, his face appeared flushed. He was new at his job as supervisor and sometimes that showed when talking to us Counselor IVs. In the beginning, he hesitated in his choice of words to say. One time during a meeting of Counselor IVs, he told us we would have to get our Master's degree within a year or we wouldn't have a job at CCAD. For me, a comment like this was devastating. My husband and I had a mortgage, a car payment, and other debt. The question I asked myself was, *How am I going to accomplish obtaining my Master's degree with all that debt?* Turning to the other three Counselor IVs, they looked equally dumbfounded by his comment. To me, he wielded his power and control over us and enjoyed doing so.

My roommate, Elaine, had gone to John Carey the second day after he started his job. She wanted to tell him in no uncertain terms that he was not to intimidate staff or inmates. Apparently, her comments fell on deaf ears. John Carey had the book "Winning Through Intimidation" down pat. He practiced intimidation in his daily life at CCAD.

The only time I saw John Carey really vulnerable was at a meeting with Counselor IVs. He shared that he had been sitting at his desk the previous morning when he had passed out on his desk. We were all concerned for him. He said he was going to go to a doctor the next day. Perhaps the pressure cooker was getting to him.

The only Counselor IV that had her act together was Lorraine. She was one of the original staff members hired back in 1989. She was a state and national certified alcohol and drug counselor. She was well versed in all aspects of the program. Lorraine also had a total recall of all facts and information pertaining to CCAD and Cripple Creek Correctional Facility. She received her degree from Eastern Colorado University and was well on her way to completing her Master's.

She didn't let John Carey intimidate her and that was her attitude and philosophy. Lorraine had worked hard to get to where she was in her career as a counselor and mentor to other counselors. She was tenacious and would fight to have her voice heard above the crowd. Who else was on the counselor team?

Frank O'Quin was soft spoken but direct in his questions he asked of John Carey of the other Counselor IVs. He loved spending a weekend riding his Harley motorcycle. He wore his feelings on his sleeve and for the most part, you knew where he stood on any particular issue being addressed or discussed at staff interchanges or counselor IV meetings. This was also his approach when dealing with inmates. He was very thankful in his comments to staff and inmates. He wore his hair in a curly perm and it was graying. He had some health issues that necessitated him being off work occasionally. Frank was pretty close to John Carey, seeing him as a mentor and role model.

The third member of the Counselor IV team was Paula. She was very bright and caring in her approach to inmates. She had previous work experience within a prison in Idaho. She was a good listener and always had thoughtful and diplomatic comments to make in regards to issues, inmates, and staff. She was very patient and you couldn't rattle her cage very easily. Paula had health issues in regards to her lungs as she was a heavy smoker and had smoked cigarettes for years. She had a new custom build home in the valley towards Haines, Colorado. She enjoyed her weekends off where she described what she liked as "veg out." Paula was a true team member and offered encouragement to the rest of the team. She was one of the first hires at CCAD. As for myself, I was very quiet. Listening and taking in comments by staff was my forte. I was driven to do my very best at whatever was assigned to me. I maintained a caseload of five inmates, supervised three counselors, and taught criminality, stress management, and self-esteem. While at a weekly Counselor IV meeting, John

Carey had asked for volunteers to do a new orientation video. I raised my hand to volunteer. My FE-2 Nikon was my baby. Photography was a real passion for me. While pursuing my passion, I had won three photography contests. I had a photograph, titled "A Gathering of Geese," in Sapporo, Japan on permanent exhibit. I only found out later that the goose was one of the lucky signs of the Japanese. The photograph was a Monet shot with three geese looking out at a pond of water. Perhaps they were thinking, *There's a hot female goose across the pond.*

Like all of the Counselor IVs, I took pride in my job and as a member of the Counselor IV team, I felt I had earned my title. I supported the Program at CCAD and I advocated for change, treatment, and recovery for inmates. This was the complete opposite of Paul's position. He supported the cause of marijuana and that marijuana shouldn't be an illegal drug. He took marijuana for his bad back and would continue to do so after being released.

MY FIRST BRIEF ENCOUNTER

My first brief encounter with Paul Patterson occurred on Wednesday, March 6, 1996. I told the inmate I needed for him to complete some initial forms/paperwork for me. He briefly argued with me.

My response was, "That's that, I don't want to discuss it any further, do you understand?"

"Yeah, sure!"

I told him I would see him in my office tomorrow at 11:00 AM. He left my office. I said to myself in a whisper, "This guy is going to be a real challenge! He obviously didn't want to be in the program."

He was 6' 1" with brownish hair and blue eyes. I noticed his hair was thinning in the back and he had shoulder length hair.

We met the next day as planned. I completed his CPMS releases of information, treatment contract, and his medical history. I explained to him that we would be meeting for at least three hours next time to complete what is called a "database." It was lengthy! Sixteen papers would take time. He asked what a database was. I was abrupt in my answer. "It is a complete social and psychological history of your life." I tore off the page with the heading CRIMINAL HISTORY at the top. I told him to complete his criminal history starting with the first crime he committed and describe in length the nature of the crime.

He asked. "What's that for? You have my complete rap sheet in your file, don't you?"

I answered by saying again, "You still need to complete the form."

And so it began, the dialogue with Paul. As I recall, the day was extremely busy as usual. I had group in the morning, a meeting with my supervisor, a mediation between clients, progress notes to complete after group, and a one-on-one with another client on my caseload. I was rushed, as usual; too much paperwork and meetings!

Group started at 8:45 AM with a feelings check. Another counselor and eight inmates were in the group. Morning group could vary in discussion and subject matter but it was basically a therapy group. We used a very confronting style to chisel away at their thinking process and denial of their alcoholism and drug addiction.

SEPTEMBER

One of the persons that I supervised needed the night off. It was a Saturday. Every Saturday, a staff member would take ten inmates to La Grande for an AA meeting that was held at the Methodist Church.

The night was one of those beautiful nights. It was warm and inviting. Before I entered the facility, I photographed the sunset. The Lord was present that night. He was with us and felt by me then and now.

So I go back to that night in September for those that wish to read this story. I speak and write the truth and everything that happened that faithful night did occur.

As I drove to La Grande, I turned the radio on to listen to some music. It was rock & roll. I felt very happy and it was good to know that Paul was behind me as I drove the van. The music made me feel even happier and free, like an open book.

In addition, I wanted to take photographs for the orientation slide presentation that I was doing for the program. This would give me that opportunity too.

The AA meeting was excellent. We stood at the beginning of the meeting saying the Serenity Prayer while holding hands. I was holding hands with Paul. A strange feeling came over my hand. I felt a real connection with Paul.

**IN THE CIRCUIT COURT OF THE STATE OF COLORADO
FOR THE COUNTY OF ADAMS**

In the Matter of the Dissolution
Of the Marriage of

Teresa Patterson

        Petitioner

And
Paul Jonah Patterson

        Respondent

Case No. 95DM0946

STIPULATED DECREE
OF DISSOLUTION
OF MARRIAGE

This matter is now ready for hearing on the merits; Petitioner appearing by her attorney, Daniel M. Hinrichs; Respondent not appearing; and the parties stipulating to a settlement of all matters; now, therefore,

It appears that the Court has jurisdiction of this matter; the allegations of the Petition are true and that irreconcilable differences of the parties have caused the irremediable breakdown of their marriage; Respondent is in default herein; and the Petitioner has filed a motion and affidavit for decree of dissolution of marriage without a hearing.

IT IS HEREBY ORDERED AND DECREED that:

1. The marriage of the parties shall terminate on the 19th day of Feb, 1996.

2. Irreconcilable differences exist between the parties which have caused the irremediable breakdown of their marriage.

3. If either party shall die before said date, the marriage shall terminate immediately before such death, unless the appeal is pending; upon such death (if an appeal is pending) the estate of the decedent shall be the nominal party and the Court of Appeals shall have the power to determine finally all matters presented on such appeal.

4. Portions of any wills of either party distributing the property to the other party antedating the date of this Decree are revoked unless the terms of the Will specifically express a contrary intention.

5. Neither party is entitled to cohabit with the other from this date hereof.

6. This Decree may be vacated within thirty (30) days of this date upon joint motion of the parties.

7. Petitioner is awarded custody of the minor children of the parties, subject to the Adams County Courts jurisdiction over the children under Case Nos. J-5645, J-5646, and J-5647 and placement of the children with the State Office for Services to Children and Families. Respondent is allowed reasonable visitation with the children upon his release from prison, subject to the terms and conditions imposed in Adams County Case Nos. J-5645, J-5646, and J-5647.

8. Commencing thirty (30) days after his release from prison, Respondent shall pay the sum of $186.00 per month as a contribution to the support of the minor children. Said monthly payments shall be made on the same day each month thereafter, until the earlier of the following events: (a) the child's emancipation; (b) the child's death; or (c) if the child is attending school as that term is defined by Colorado law the child's attainment of age twenty one (21) years; but if the child is not attending school as that term is defined by Colorado law, the child's attainment of the age eighteen (18) years. Said payments shall be made through the Department of Human Resources, Child Support Program, P.O. Box 14506, Denver, Colorado 80123.

Petitioner herein requests the collection, accounting, disbursement and enforcement services provided by the Department of Human Resources and Respondent shall make payments through the Department of Human Resources.

NOTICE OF INCOME WITHHOLDING

The support order is enforceable by income withholding under S 2, 3, and 5 to 20 of this 1993 Act. Withholding shall occur immediately, whenever there are arrearages at least equal to the support payment for one month, whenever the obligated parent requests such withholding or whenever the oblige requests withholding for good cause. The district attorney or, as appropriate, the Support Enforcement Division of the Department of Justice will assist in securing such withholding. Exceptions may apply in some circumstances.

Payment of support under a new or modified order shall be by income withholding and an exception of income withholding may be granted under the provisions of S9 of Chapter 796, Colorado Laws 1993.

9. Respondent shall maintain health insurance for the minor children of the parties so long as it is available through his place of employment. The parties shall each pay one-half of all medical, dental, orthodontic and any and all other health expenses incurred on behalf of the children of the parties which are not covered by insurance.

10. The Note and Trust Deed for the sale of the parties' residence and real property shall be sold to a broker, with the proceeds distributes as follows:

(a) All outstanding credit card bills of approximately $8,000.00 shall be paid off.

(b) Balance of the proceeds shall be divided equally between the parties.

11. The parties' 1993 Terry Resort 30-foot travel trailer, VIN 1EA1S2928P245004, shall be sold and the proceeds divided equally between them.

12. Petitioner is awarded the 1988 Dodge Shadow, subject to any encumbrances thereon and free from any claims of Respondent.

13. Respondent is awarded the 1983 CJ5, license plate #LUVMUD, subject to any encumbrances thereon and free from any claims of Petitioner.

14. Respondent is specifically awarder the following personal property:

        (a) Chainsaw
        (b) Bose speakers
        (c) His personal papers
        (d) His clothes
        (e) Miscellaneous tools

The above items are to be picked up by Lon Sweet within thirty (30) days of the date of this decree.

15. Except as otherwise specifically set forth above, the parties are each awarded all personal property currently in their possession.

16. The parties are each responsible for their own individual debts incurred since August, 1995, and shall hold each other harmless therefrom.

17. Each party shall sign all documents necessary to effect a transfer of ownership of the personal property. Each party is responsible for, and shall hold the other party harmless from, any encumbrances on any property awarded to that party.

18. Petitioner's maiden name of Teresa Matthews is hereby restored.

19. Relevant data is as follows:

HUSBAND: Paul Jonah Patterson

Residence: Arrowhead Correctional Center,
          57500 US-50, Canon City, Colorado 81212

Age: 40   Date of Birth: 09/15/55

Social Security No.:

WIFE: Teresa Matthews Patterson

Residence: P.O. Box 35, Cripple Creek, CO 80813

Age: 34   Date of Birth: 09/31/61

Social Security No.:

Maiden Name: Matthews   Former Married Names: None

MONEY JUDGMENT (Child Support)

Judgment Creditor:

Judgment Creditor's Attorney: Daniel M. Hinrichs

Judgment Debtor:

Amount: $186.00 per month
                      commencing 30 days after
                      Respondent's release from prison.

Interest: Simple interest accrues on
                      any arrearages.

Dated this 19th day of Jan, 1996.

                              CIRCUIT JUDGE
                              ROBERT F. WALBERG

IT IS SO STIPULATED:

Teresa Patterson   Paul J. Patterson
Petitioner   Respondent
Date: _____   Date: _12-19-95_

DANIEL M. HINRICHS (92591)
Attorney for Petitioner
Date: _1/16/96_

COLORADO CHILD SUPPORT CALCULATOR

Adams County Circuit Court #95DM0946
        PETITIONER
        RESPONDENT

	Min-Wag	$4.75	$823
CHILDREN'S NAMES	CHILDREN		Date-Birth
	1		12/21/86
	2		08/04/90
	3		03/16/94
	4		
	5		
	6		

	Custodial	Non Custod.
B1 MONTHLY GROSS INCOME--------------------→	823	823
B2 Alimony received (+) or paid (-) ---------------→	0	0
Subtotal gross income--------------------------→	823	823
No. of joint children for whom support sought ->	3	3
No. of non-joint children in parent's home------→	0	0
# of non-jt. childr. for whom supt. Ordered ----→	0	0
A2 Total non-joint children (not stepchildren) -----→	0	0
B4 credit Support for Total non-joint children ------→	0	0
B5 Adjusted Gross Monthly Income -----------------→	823	823
B6 Each Parents % of Adjusted Gross Income ------→	50.00%	50.00%
B7 SUPPORT form lookup table (both parents) -----→	372	372
B7A Work related child care costs -------------------→	0	0
Subtract calculated child care credit -----------→	0	0
B7B Recurring medical expenses --------------------→	0	0
B7C Total adjustment to basic support -------------→	0	0
B8 TOTAL Child Support Obligation (both parents) -→	372	372
Each parents child support obligation -----------→	186	186
B10 Presumed Child Support Obligation ------------→		186
B11 Cost of health ins. for joint-children only ------→	0	0
B12 Portion of insurance added or deducted -------→	0	0
B13 TOTAL PRESUMED SUPPORT ORDER-------------------------------→		186

In the Circuit Court of the State of Colorado

For __Adams__ County_____
                      (If Family Law Department, so state)

SUPPORT ORDER ABSTRACT

Petitioner: _____Teresa Patterson_____

Address: _____P.O. Box 35_____

Cripple Creek, CO_____ Zip Code 80813__

SS#_____ Birthdate _09/34/61_ Sex _F_

This is:
X A new order (enter A thru C)
   A modification (enter A thru E)

THIS ORDER:

A. Case No. 95DM0946

B. Date of Order:
   _____

C. Type of Proceedings:

Dissolution of Marriage

Respondent: Paul Jonah Patterson

Address: Arrowhead Correctional Center

57500 US-50 Canon City, CO Zip Code 81212

SS# _____ Birthdate _09/15/55_ Sex _M_

ORIGINAL ORDER:

D. County: _____

E. Case No. _____

Date/Place of Marriage: Carson City County, Nevada; May 15, 1983

Date/Place when Separated: Adams County, Colorado; August, 1995

Obligor* (person to make payments):

Obligor's Employer's Name/Address:

Payment $ _186.00_   Frequency monthly   First Due Date _*_

Arrearage Amount _____

BENEFICIARY(IES) (FIRST NAMES ONLY)	BIRTH DATE	RELATIONSHIP	SOCIAL SECURITY NO.
		Son	
		Son	
		Daughter	

AMOUNT	OBLIGATION EXPIRATION DATE
62.00	COS 107.108
62.00	COS 107.108
62.00	COS 107.108

*Respondent's support obligation is to commence 30 days after his release from prison (Special Distribution Required)

CRIMINAL AUTOBIOGRAPHY—Paul Patterson

CRIME #1
Petty Theft: Stole cigarettes from Safeway
- I. Masks Used
  - A. "Good Guy"
  - B. "Naïve Ned"
  - C. "The Victim"
  - D. "Hope Fiend"

- A. "Good Guy": I used this mask as a means to be accepted by criminal peers. Also used the mask as part of my portrayal of being a victim of my peers and their ideas.
- B. "Naïve Ned": I used this mask to try and convince the store clerk that I has never done anything like this before. And that the older guys told me that the store would just let me go.
- C. "The Victim": I used this mask to try and convince the clerk hat some guys were going to beat me up if I didn't come in the store and steal some cigarettes.
- D. "Hope Fiend": I used this mask around my criminal friends because it was important to me to be accepted by this group. I was young and thought of criminal activity as a glorifying experience and sought out that excitement and acceptance.

#16--Lying: I also remember lying to the store clerk, store manager and city police officer. I told them I didn't have a telephone at home, in hopes that they would let me go.
#19—Victim Stance: I immediately blamed my friends for talking me into this irrational behavior.
#22 Failure to Consider Injury to Others: I didn't consider the injury to myself, much less others—stores have insurance.
#29—Lack of Interest in Responsible Performance: To have acted responsible and walked away instead of going along with the idea would have looked uncool and would not have served my distorted needs and beliefs.
#32—Poor Decision Making for Responsible Living: I never once considered anything remotely "responsible" in the decision to commit this act of thievery.
#33—Cutoff: As with my decision process, I don't believe I ever considered anything other than committing this crime & how to accomplish it. One deterrent was that I got caught. My dad was going to beat me severely but I do not recall considering this consequence, so if I did, it was only for a fleeting moment.

CRIME #2
- I. Masks Used
  - A. "Good Guy"
  - B. "Naïve Ned"
  - C. "Puppet Master"
  - D. "Sarcastic Sam"

- A. "Good Guy": I tried to project this image to my parents and law enforcement officers. Pure manipulation in order to get away with and continue my criminal activities.
- B. "Naïve Ned": This mask was used to claim my innocence—to portray myself as law abiding and innocent. "I would never dream of taking someone else's car...I don't even know how to drive a car."

C. "Puppet Master": I always believed that I was not only above the law but much smarter than the officers who enforce it. I believed that the average person could not catch me stealing their car. Every time I stole someone's car, I felt in control, and that I was making fools out of the car owners. Concerned only with my own selfish desires: a ride.

D. "Sarcastic Sam": I would steal cars and drive them up to school for an attention getter. To be the center of attention...thinking about how ignorant the police were.

II. Crime

Grand Theft Auto (this is a cluster)
Stole numerous cars from all over the city, used cars for transportation to parties and from home, to friend's houses. Did this for kicks and attention.

III. Thinking Errors Used

Energy, Pride, Power-thrust, Concrete Thinking, Uniqueness, Lying, Lack of Time Perspective, Failure to Put Oneself in Another's Position, Failure to Consider Injury to Others, Lack of Interest in Responsible Performance, Failure to Endure Adversity, Poor Decision Making for Responsible Living, Cutoff, Sure Optimism.

Energy: I used energy as a thinking error when I was not able to live within my reality. I could have used the bus, walked, or hitch-hiked, but that was boring to me. One day someone showed me how to steal a car and I found that exciting. I took pride in my ability to steal cars and not get caught. I took pride in long I could keep a car without getting caught.

Power Thrust: It was for me doing the forbidden and getting away with it...pure excitement for me.

Concrete Thinking: I would tell myself that I had to have a car to get around on Friday and Saturday nights. I would tell myself that it was cool and crazy. I thought that people/peers liked this about me.

Uniqueness: I believed that I was unique in the idea that I was so good I would never get caught. Plus I thought being a car thief in itself was unique.

Lying: I lied to some people about whether the car they were riding in was stolen or not. I lied to the police about how many cars I had stolen and whether I was alone or not. I lied to my parents about my stealing the cars the police had asked about.

Lack of Time Perspective: I wanted a car and I wanted it now. Most of my peers were getting cars for their birthdays or were working and saving their money to buy themselves a car. Me? I wasn't going to get a car from my folks nor could I save a nickel. So I stole what I wanted.

Failure to Put Oneself in Another's Position: I failed to consider the risk of those I gave rides to. I never considered the impact on those whose cars I stole, or what I would feel like if I was the one missing my car. I never considered the impact on the police.

IV. Obstruction Tactics Used

A. Telling others what they want to hear and not what is truth: I used this tactic when I was giving rides to girls, friends, strangers (hitch-hikers) because I led everyone (those who didn't know about my criminal activities) to believe the cars were mine. I also used this tactic when questioned by the police and my parents.

       B.   Lying—by Omission: I used this tactic when questioned by the police and parents. Also used it when giving girls rides, or while on a date.

V. Feelings at the time
      A.   Victims:
          Car Owners:
          Aggravated/Angry/Bitter/Demoralized/Depressed/Deprived/Disr egarded/Distraught/Emotional/Enraged/Frustrated Hostile/Hysterical/Irritated/Intimidated/Miserable/Outraged/ Provoked/Resentful/Robbed
          Police:
          Aggravated/Frustrated/Irritated/Provoked/Resentful/ Powerful
          Parents:
          Shamed/Stunned/Annoyed/Frustrated/Powerless/ Humiliated/Infuriated/Irritated/Emotional/Hostile/Embarrassed/ Depressed/Disappointed/Discouraged/Disgraced/Dissatisfied/ Disturbed/Concerned/Angry/Aggravated/Shocked/Annoyed/ Offended/Defeated/Ignored
          General Public:
          Violated/Affected/Disregarded/Frustrated/Angry

      B.   My Feelings:
          Adventurous/Accepted/Aggressive/Arrogant/Ashamed/Brave/ Challenged/Afraid/Daring/Depressed/Disgraced/Discouraged/ Disappointment/Emotional/Loyal/Fearful/Frightened/Miserable/ Horrible/Hateful/Humiliated/Stupid/Rebellious/Reckless/ Remorseful

VI. Victims
      A.   Who were my victims?
          Store clerk, store manager, Safeway corp., police officer, taxpayers, community, mother, father, myself
      B.   Victims of my thinking, feelings, behavior
          Same as listed above (starting in reverse with me listed first)

CRIME #3

I.   Masks
    A.   "Good Guy"
    B.   "Naïve Ned"
    C.   "The Victim"

A.   "Good Guy": I used this mask to get what I needed from those around me. I used it to look good around my parents. All the while I was committing crimes on my home front. I used this mask to con a detective into letting me go, without bail, on the pretense that I would help him recover more stolen property.
B.   'Naïve Ned": I used this mask in conjunction with the idea I could manipulate the District Attorney. I played on the idea that I was just a low-on-the-totem-pole dope fiend and it was unknown to me that this property was stolen.

II. Crime
     Receiving Stolen Property
     Possession of Paraphernalia
These charges were the result of my selling drugs/heroin. I sold drugs to support my own drug habit and for profit. I would trade drugs for stolen property if it was something I wanted or could make a profit from.

III. Thinking Errors Used
     Suggestibility: To get caught. I could do heroin and not get addicted
     The Loner: It was me against everyone. People who tried to get close to me, I ran off. It was my past experience that the least amount of people who knew what I was up to, the safer I was there was hardly room for my S.O. in this life style.
     Lying: I lied to everyone: my parents, my S.O., my associates, my customers, etc. This was an effective way to keep my life secretive and keep me in control—at least that was my belief at the time.
     "I can't": When thinking things were going sour, I would want to get out of this business and I would want to quit doing heroin. I would always end up telling myself, "I can't" and would continue to do the same activities.
     Failure to put oneself in another's position: I never looked at life or my actions from the perspective of anyone but myself. I was a negative aspect of all those whose lives my life touched...I was totally oblivious to the impact.
     Failure to consider injury to others: I hurt a lot of people with my inappropriate behavior. I hurt people (my parents, my S.O., the neighbors, the community, customers) by supplying drugs that tore people's lives apart or impacted them in one negative way or another. I never considered this at the time. I was only interested in myself.
     Corrosion and Cutoff: I believe that my desire to be accepted by my S.O. (at that time) was a major factor in my corrosion. She wanted me to experiment with heroin and told me that I would love it. I wanted her and to be accepted by her...so I threw common sense to the wind. Cut off took place when I discovered that there was money to be made and free drugs to do. This put me in "Sugar Daddy" status with my S.O.
     Deferment: What fits for me is the idea that someday I would quit this lifestyle and settle down...and that was always put off until tomorrow.

IV. Obstruction Tactics Used
     A. Telling others what they want to hear and not what is truth. I use this tactic to survive as a criminal.
     B. Lying by omission: I used this tactic with the police, my girlfriend, my parents, customers, and, more than likely, myself. At some point or another, I told myself what I was doing was alright/okay—in fact lying to myself.

V. Feelings at the time
     A. Victims:
     Parents:
     Shamed/Stunned/Annoyed/Frustrated/Powerless/Humiliated/
     Infuriated/Irritated/Emotional/Hostile/Embarrassed/Depressed/
     Disappointed/Discouraged/Disgraced/Dissatisfied/Disturbed/
     Concerned/Angry

VI. Victims/Who were my victims?
   A.   Myself
   B.   Girlfriend
   C.   Courts
   D.   Community/Neighbors
   E.   Police
   F.   Dog
   G.   Parents

CRIME #4

   I. Masks
   A. "Good Guy"
   B. "Illiterate Dummy"
   C. "Tough Guy"

   A.   "Good Guy": I always use this mask when I'm selling drugs or in the
        presence of those I wish to deceive/manipulate. A back-stabber in the
        sense that I would take advantage of you if you gave me the
        opportunity.
   B.   "Illiterate Dummy": I used this mask as a tactic. Scheming to get my
        way or to manipulate someone. Used it against fellow drug dealers,
        customers, the police, courts, etc.
   C.   "Tough Guy": I used this mask by being aggressive both in sales and
        purchases of illicit drugs. I also did it to keep people from hanging on
        me—fair-weather friends.

   II. Crime
        Possession of a controlled substance (a variety of pharmaceutical uppers
        and downers)

   III. Thinking Errors Used

Suggestibility: I was very suggestible to anyone's ideas if I thought it would be
exciting, or of benefit to me...like make me feel good or look good.
Failure to consider injury to others: As usual, I never consider anyone. Even in
my criminal past, I thought there were times when I considered myself but
looking back, that appears to be a very distorted view on my part. I never looked
at the impact of the drugs I sold on other people's lives and their families...the
serious potential of death and destruction.
Failure to assume responsible initiatives: To have assumed a responsible initiative
would have been contrary to my beliefs. It would have been to find socially
acceptable means of having fun and making money, to be willing to live within my
means and be humble.
Failure to endure adversity: This thinking error works hand in hand with the
failure to assume responsible initiatives. To be humble and live within my own
means is to deal with adversity. To meet life on life's terms is to endure
adversity. Making money and doing drugs illegally is avoiding life and its common
everyday struggle. I was unwilling to even consider anything but what I wanted
and the shortest way to get there.
Poor decision making for responsible living: Since I was living in my own distorted

V. Feelings at the time
  A. Victims:
     Parents:
     Shamed/Stunned/Annoyed/Frustrated/Powerless/Humiliated/
     Infuriated/Irritated/Emotional/Hostile/Embarrassed/Depressed/
     Disappointed/Discouraged/Disgraced/Dissatisfied/Disturbed/
     Concerned/Angry
     Neighborhood/Community:
     Affected/Aggravated/Angry/Challenged/Callous/Combative/Concerned/
     Defensive/Determined/Disgusted/Distressed/Fearful/Frustrated/Hostile/
     Infuriated/Intimidated/Irritated/Optimistic/Out-raced/Powerful
     Police:
     Aggravated/Frustrated/Irritated/Provoked/Resentful/Powerful
     General Public/Tourists:
     Affected/Annoyed/Complacent/Complaining/Disappointed/Disgusted/
     Disturbed/Emotional/Enraged/Fearful/Frustrated/Involved/Infuriated/
     Intimidated
     Customers:
     Self-Destructive/Regretful/Uneasy/Cautious/Risky/Anxious/Important
     /Accepted/Valued/Apprehensive/Clever/Cold/Complacent/Confused/
     Cool/Daring/Dependent/Depressed/Desperate/Destructive/
     Disappointed/Discouraged/Disgusted/Doubtful/Down/Dreary/
     Emotional/Enthused/Envious/Excited/Greedy/Helpless/Happy
     /Frustrated/Foolish

  B. My feelings:
      Adventurous/Aggressive/Betrayed/Bitter/Boastful/Carefree/Careless
      /Clever/Cold/Confident/Crazy/Daring/Deceitful/Destructive/
      Distrustful/Embarrassed

  I. Masks
    A. Square Dope Fiend

  A. "Dope Fiend": Is part of my make up in order to deceive the police,
      my neighbors, my landlord, straight friends, and other dope fiends
      that I didn't want to be discovered by.

  II. Crime
       Cultivation of marijuana, Child neglect, Assault with intent to do
       great bodily harm.
       Growing marijuana on the side of my cabin drew the attention of a
       neighbor's 17 year old son. He attempted to steal my plants in the
       middle of the night. He got caught by me and was assaulted,
       physically. This is a cluster of "manufacture" crimes.

  III. Thinking Errors Used
       Energy, The Power Thrust, Sentimentality, Uniqueness, The Loner,
       The Victim Stance, Lack of Time Perspective, Failure to Put Oneself
       in Another's Position, Failure to Consider Injury to Others, Failure to
       Assume Responsible Initiatives, Lack of Interest in Responsible
       Performance, Poor Decision-Making for Responsible Living, Corrosion
       and Cutoff, Super-optimism.

Energy: I'm always seeking excitement. I find growing marijuana very exciting and rewarding. The same feelings that one obtains from growing vegetables in a garden. It was exciting when I heard someone outside my cabin in the middle of the night...the thought of catching someone and ruffing them up was exciting too.

Lack of time perspective: I never experienced being happy with where I am in life. Always wanting more and wanting it immediately...this was part of the reason for growing pot—money and more money.

The power thrust: I find growing and selling marijuana very exciting with respect to getting money from it.

Sentimentality: I would think about the money and how I was going to spend it. Planning the future was the focus of my criminal activity. I used my sentimentality as a cover to hide my criminal intentions.

Uniqueness: I thought I was slicker and better than most growers. This made me feel good when I got away to go to my grow operation—that allowed me to believe I was unique. I felt unique when I believed that the kid I hit was not going to tell on me for breaking his arm because he was actually in the commission of a crime.

The loner: In order to carry out my crimes and lessen the risk of getting caught I had to lead a very secretive life. Keeping people away to avoid exposure and accountability.

The victim stance: I immediately blame the kid, who was stealing the plants, for my getting arrested. Never taking ownership for the fact that it was my criminal acts (growing) that attracted this kid to my property.

Lack of time perspective: It's my opinion that "shortcuts" are essential.

Failure to put oneself in another's position: I didn't consider anyone in regards to me committing crimes. I didn't think about the boy or the boy's parents in regards to the hospital bills. Never considering the impact on those who bought my pot—money spent on "smoke". POOF!

Failure to consider injury to others: This is the other half of the above thinking error. I didn't consider the harm that I caused those around me. Customers, myself, parents, victim's parents, the landlord, the police, the community, etc. I considered only myself.

Failure to assume responsible initiatives: Being responsible would have meant for me to wait for my wants. It would have required me to stop using and selling and manufacturing drugs. It would have required me to accept and deal with my feeling each and every day, instead of avoiding them by medicating myself.

Lack of interest in responsible performance: I never consider being responsible with consideration for the laws and rights of others. I wasn't responsible when it came to my own well-being. I wanted to be an outlaw and play cops and robbers instead of being a responsible man. Never considering my past or future.

Poor decision making for responsible living: The decision to grow marijuana for a means to make money was a poor decision on my part. Protecting my marijuana with a baseball bat was a poorer decision. And making a decision to hit someone with the intent to do great harm was a decision which was insult to injury.

Corrosion and cutoff: There were many opportunities to change. Many opportunities to stop my illegal behavior. But I would continue to talk myself into believing that what I did was okay, even necessary. Always casting caution away, common sense thrown to the wind.

Super-optimism: Anything I chose to do is a done deal. That's been my attitude about growing marijuana. Never allowing myself to doubt that I could and would get away with my criminal activities...absolute confidence.

IV. Obstruction Tactics Used

To keep my actions secretive, also telling others what they want to hear and not what is the truth: I would tell my parents that I was being good and not drugging or breaking the law.

Lying by omission: I could not afford to tell anyone the truth about what I did when people were not around. A Dr. Jekyll/Mr. Hyde personality is required to grow marijuana and be deceptive about it.

Silence: This tactic is necessary for criminals.

Vagueness: I would only tell what was necessary when being confronted by police. I never volunteered information about my past or where I was from, or if I had been arrested before.

Minimize the situation: I did this when I talked to my folks on the phone trying to post bail. I would tell them that I got arrested for growing marijuana but I wouldn't let on that there were other charges—like "assault" or possession of other drugs, etc.

V. Feelings at the time

A. Victims:

Parents:

Affected/Aggravated/Angry/Annoyed/Betrayed/Bewildered/Callous/Caring/Cheated/Combative/Concerned/Deceived/Depressed/Desperate/Determined/Disappointed/Discouraged/Disgusted/Distrustful/Drained/Embarrassed/Emotional/Frustrated/Hurt/Imposed Upon/Infuriated/Insulted/Irritated/Let Down/Loving/Miserable/Perplexed/Powerless/Reluctant/Resentful/Shocked/Skeptical/Etc.

Parents of Assault Victim:

Shook Up/Shocked/Sickened/Revengeful/Resentful/Provoked/Malicious/Miserable/Irritated/Infuriated/Hysterical/Hostile/Horrified/Hateful/Frustrated/Emotional/Distressed/Defensive/Concerned/Cold/Cheated/Bitter/Annoyed/Angry/Aggravated/Aggressive

Victim:

Adventurous/Afraid/Aggressive/Agony/Angry/Ashamed/Bitter/Capable/Cautious/Daring/Defensive/Depressed/Disappointed/Disgraced/Embarrassed/Emotional/Fearful/Foolish/Frightened/Helpless/Horrified/Hostile/Hurt/Hysterical/Intimidated/Mischievious/Miserable/Pain/Powerful/Powerless/Reckless/Resentful/Revengeful/Terrified/Vulnerable

Children:

Affected/Afraid/Angry/Annoyed/Apprehensive/Cheated/Concerned/Confused/Curious/Deceived/Defensive/Depressed/Deprived/Despair/Disappointed/Dominated/Doubtful/Embarrassed/Emotional/Fear/Forgiving/Frightened/Grief/Guilty/Hateful/Helpless/Homesick/Horrified/Hurt/Insecure/Isolated/Let Down/Mixed Up/Overwhelmed/Powerless/Remorseful/Scared/Stunned/Threatened/Tricked/Uncertain/Uncomfortable/Unhappy/Vulnerable/Worried

Wife:

Adored/Adventurous/Affected/Affectionate/Afraid/Aggravated/Agreeable/Agony/Ambitious/Angry/Annoyed/Anxious/Appreciative/Apprehensive/Argumentative/Asserting/Attractive/Bewildered/Bitchy/Bitter/Burdened/Caring/Cautious/Cheated/Clever/Complacent/Cooperative/Daring/Defensive/Deceitful/Dependant/Depressed/Dreary/Embarrassed/Emotional/Enraged/Exhausted/Exuberant/Fear/Forgiving/Foolish/Good/Greedy/Helpful/Helpless/Horrified/Hostile/Humiliated/Hurt/Hysterical/Impressed/

Interested/Involved/Joyous/Let Down/Loving/Miserable/Motherly/
Optimistic/Overwhelmed/Panic/Patient/Peaceful/Persecuted/Pleased/
Powerful/Powerless/Pressured/Pull Apart/Resourceful/Responsible/
Revengeful/Sad/Safe/Sarcastic/Satisfied/Scared/Self-Centered/
Threatened/Trusting/Troubled/Vulnerable/Unhappy/Happy
Police, Courts, Community:
Affected/Aggravated/Aggressive/Alert/Angry/Annoyed/Apprehensive
/Bitter/Burdened/Callous/Capable/Caring/Cautious/Challenged/
Combative/Competent/Concerned/Confident/Defensive/Deceived/
Deprived/Determined/Dignified/Disappointed/Distrustful/
Embarrassed/Emotional/Fearful/Forceful/Good/Gratified/Happy/
Humorless/Idealistic/Impatient/Important/Infuriated/Intimidated/
Intolerant/Irritated/Knowledgeable/Logical/Loyal/Offended/Opposed
/Outraged/Persistent/Powerful/Powerless/Provoked/Proud/
Rational/Realistic/Resentful/Resourceful/Respected/Responsible/
Responsive/Regarded/Righteous/Satisfied/Secretive/Serious/
Shocked/Sophisticated/Stern/Suspicious/Threatened/Tricked/
Unhappy/Useful/Valued/Vulnerable

B. My feelings:
Adventurous/Aggressive/Betrayed/Boastful/Careless/Clever/Daring/
Caring/Confident/Crazy/Deceitful/Destructive/Constructive/
Distrustful (Authority)/Embarrassed/Emotional/Evil/Fearful/
Paranoid/Foolish/Stupid/Guilty/Hard-Headed/Stubborn/Angry/
Happy/Powerful/Powerless/Loved/Needed/Important/Loving/
Concerned/Proud/Resentful/Cautious/Criminal!!

VI. Victims/ Who were my victims?
Parents and Parents of Assault Victims
Assault Victim
Children
Wife
Police
Courts
Public
Community
Neighborhood
Customer
Myself

CRIME #5

I. Masks
A. "Naïve Ned"
B. "Sentimental Sam"
C. "The Victim"
D. "Square Dope Fiend"

A. "Naïve Ned": is used as a means to cover up what I'm attempting to do in regards to criminal behavior, portraying someone innocent and law abiding.

B. "Sentimental Sam": is also a part of this image, drawing in neighbors as friends so as to look like Joe citizen...they would tell others how nice a boy I was...all the while planning and partaking in crime.

C. "The Victim": I used this mask as a means to gain some sympathy from the courts and my victim's parents.

D. "Square Dope Fiend": ...

II. Crime
My behavior was both the selling of these drugs and the use of them myself.

III. Thinking Errors Used
Energy, Pride, Power Thrust, Concrete Thinking, Suggestibility, Failure to Consider Injury to Others, Failure to Assume Responsible Initiatives, Lack of Trust, Lack of Interest in Responsible Performance, Failure to Endure Adversity, Poor Decision Making for Responsible Living, Cutoff.

Energy: I use energy as a thinking error fundamentally to make it okay with myself to do my crime, constantly looking for excitement.

Pride: I took pride in selling and possessing the best drugs. I also took pride in making money and having money.

Power Thrust: Again, I used this thinking error in respect to the excitement of selling drugs and getting away with it. With drugs, I could control people and feel powerful, wanted and needed.

Concrete Thinking: My belief that this was the way to gain my happiness was very concrete in my mind. The idea was that nothing else would make me feel good or wanted.

Suggestibility: I was suggestible to my own suggestive thoughts, such as "I could make lots of money" and "I am too slick to get caught."

Failure to consider injury to others: I didn't care of think about anyone, not even the harm to me—most of the time.

Failure to assume responsible initiatives: The responsible thing to do would have been to stoop selling and using drugs but I never allowed myself to do that. I tried to quit several times by medical treatment (detox) but I would return to the drug scene...time and time again...lost and confused and irresponsible.

Lack of trust: I trusted no one! Not even myself at times. But I would want my parents to trust me. Or I would want fellow drug users to trust me.

Lack of interest in responsible performance: The only thing I really tried to stop was using heroin, and it was usually because it was someone else's idea. It was when I had a desire in my heart to say that I did...the desire was to stay alive.

Failure to Endure Adversity: This is basically a failure to endure life on life's terms and not mine, at least that's how I see it. Living within my own, honest means has never been a reality for me.

Poor decision making for responsible living: I felt that I was being responsible to myself. A very distorted belief, which I can see today but could not back then. Like making enough money so I didn't need to apply and rely on food stamps was, to me, making a responsible decision.

Cutoff: This goes hand in hand with being a drug dealer. Never considering the total consequences...ignoring the risk to an extent...I figured I was smarter than the police.

IV. Obstruction tactics used

    A. Building myself up by putting others down: I always put myself above others...my drugs were better, my prices were better, etc.

    B. Telling others what they want to hear and now what is truth: I would tell customers to wait for me and I would be late. I tell them anything in order to get their money.

    C. Silence: I would keep secrets form people in regards to what, where, and when about my drug deals. I would not talk to police about who I was or where the drugs came from.

    D. Lying by omission: This tactic is used in everyday life as a drug dealer, also with the police.

V. Feelings at the time

    A. Victims:
    Neighborhood/Community:
    Affected/Aggravated/Angry/Challenged/Callous/Combative/
    Concerned/Defensive/Determined/Disgusted/Distressed/Fearful/
    Frustrated/Hostile/Infuriated/Intimidated/Irritated/Optimistic/
    Outraged/Powerful
    Police:
    Aggravated/Frustrated/Irritated/Provided/Resentful/Powerful
    Girlfriend:
    Self-Disgust/Soul Searching/Self-Destructive/Afraid/Angry/
    Apprehensive/Cheated/Bewildered/Confused/Complacent/
    Damned/Daring/Dependent/Distressed/Emotional/Fear/
    Forgiving/Frustrated/Mixed-up/Optimistic/Reckless/Rebellious/
    Revengeful/Strung Out/Troubled/Vulnerable
    Dog:
    Brokenhearted/Abandoned/Confused/Lost

    B. My feelings:
    Adventurous/Aggressive/Ambitious/Annoyed/Apprehensive/
    Arrogant/Betrayed/Challenged/Clever/Daring/Deceitful/
    Determined/Distrustful/Embarrassed/Emotional/Frustrated/
    Foolish/Grief (dog)/Hard-headed/Loyal/Intimidated/Irritated/
    Mean/Sorry (parents)/Tricked

VI. Victims/ Who were my victims?
    Parents
    Police
    Community
    Neighbors
    Customers
    Girlfriend
    Dog
    Myself

A NOTE ABOUT PAUL'S CRIMINAL AUTOBIOGRAPHY

It is interesting and worth mentioning that Paul left out any mention of his most serious crime, the one that brought him to prison...

LETTERS

Paul sends Amber four letters. The first letter was hand delivered by one of the counselors Amber supervised. They deliver it to her home.

In his letter to Amber, he promises to return to Adams. Enclosed in the letter is a small slip of paper with the word "Eternity" on it. The slip of paper was cut out of the magazine, "Vanity Fair." Eternity is a fragrance by Estee Lauder.

Dear Amber,

Hey! I'll bet this letter comes as a surprise...a nice one I hope. Sure do miss you around here, and your attention.

Suppose we should get to the heart of the reason I have my pen in hand. There are many reasons, but this is specific to you and your carrier. Staff isn't saying a whole lot...very tight lipped but I have experienced the camp building going on Mr. Thomas questioned me today about our one-on-ones. I told him that the rumors about us were just that—rumors. I told him point blank that he would not get any cooperation from me in regards to building a camp/case against you. My lips are sealed and you could take that to the bank.

You need—better listen real good—you need to come back and act as professional as possible. You need to appear to be very focused on your job, as a counselor and a team leader. You can be whomever you wish when you are home, but while you are at this facility you must be the Mrs. Ferguson of "yesteryear." Showing no favoritism to me or anyone. Focusing on the work required of you as a counselor. No more self-discloser, no more being overly niche ot me or anyone. I fear for your welfare and your carrier if you do not put on a ridged, professional mask when you are here. Please listen and heed those words.

This is important, too! I would like to write to you and have you do the same to me. We need an address other than your home...a friend or a P.O. Box #. I can't use your real name...I would like to call you Annie (short for Susanne) for now if that is okay with you? How about Annie Godwill (God's will). Works for me if it works for you. Remember that you must not talk about anything that would give them a clue of who you are...they read the letters. Sweetheart, I love cards...you know, funny ones, loving ones, pretty ones, sexy ones. If I got one every day it would never be to many.

After I get out of here, I will return to Adams within a few days. You can plan on that...I am.

Remember to act appropriately when you get back to work...no special attention—strictly business—that doesn't mean be mean to be either...remember that this serves your needs over time...be careful.

Chapter 5

"Three Remaining Letters Sent to Amber from Paul—dated November 4, 16, and Dec. 9, 1996"

Paul begins to change. His outlook on life is descriptive and revealing. In one sentence he tells her that he loves her and in another sentence he discounts his love toward Amber.

Change Begins for Paul-November 4, 1996

Dear Mrs. Ferguson,

Amber, I'm not sure how to say what I have to say, without hurting your feelings. I must apologize for misleading you and not protesting my feelings to you sooner.

First off, I did not write right away because I was very mad about what took place at CSP. I told you point blank in your office that I was and am committed to another person. I also told you that I was not sure that things were said and done between me and my ex-wife. You have totally ignored my position and my feelings. I did not want to hurt your feelings and did not press the issue. You had far too much authority over me and I wasn't about to piss you off. I figured I would placate you by being nice until I graduated...Figuring that we would probably never meet again. I realized that in the body of the letter I wrote you I said "I love you" but not like the love you profess to me in your letters and to others verbally. I love you as a person, not in-love with you though...does this make sense?...there is a major difference. I was really attracted to your spirituality...and you're seeming to be reborn a Christian. I was in awe by the change in you...but that is as far as my feelings go.

Now in regards to sexual advances and over tones, I hope you can see that if you put a woman in front of a man who has been incarcerated for a couple years, and she starts making physical passes, that a real man is going to respond. This is called lust not love. No matter how you add it up, it's not love. I also want you to know that I said that I would return to Adams and I fully intended to do so, but not in the way of permanent, or to get married, or anything close to that. I told you that if things didn't work out for me that I would come see you. I told you that you could in fact count on my returning to Adams but that does not mean anything other than that...I'm very sorry if you felt that this meant we were going to dive into a relationship...I told John Carey this very same thing when they questioned me about our relationship. I told him you had never expressed that to me...I read all of your letters and felt that they were very dear. I also read where you thought Amber Patterson was the perfect name. I did not respond in hopes that you would become disenchanted...but that hasn't seemed to work. And now I find myself writing a letter that I know is upsetting to you, but at some point you have to come to understand that I'm not in love with you...I'm sorry. You have left me no alternative.

I'm once again very upset that you would think it was appropriate to contact my parents. That is a very big assumption on your part...and you know what they say about assuming—correct. You are being so overbearing that I cannot breathe. If anything, this and these things/actions have pushed me far away from you...I am not "gumby" who you can mold into what you want...that does not work and that's not love either...that's "possessiveness"...far from and interacting relationship. I wanted to be friends and even possibly intimate friends but at this point you have me very upset and afraid of what you might do next.

The time you wrote about going to court and getting possession of my children scared the shit out of me. This is something that I told you I would not consider doing unless absolutely necessary. You seem to only hear what suits you...or you would already know what I've said.

I guess what I'm saying is that this would not work out for us and I sincerely apologize for not setting you straight from the beginning. Please do not write me any more letters and I do not wish to see you when I get released. Please try to understand. Take care of yourself and remember: God walks with you. I'm truly sorry.

Sincerely,

Paul

November 16, 1996

Dear Amber,
Hello!
I cannot believe I'm actually doing this...writing to you again. This is my cell mate's idea. He seems to think you deserve such a letter or a response. I myself am still stuck on my anger..."example—28 days in the bucket, 28 days loss of privileges, and a $100.00 fine..." My Christmas money at that. You actually told me that you felt I should thank you for your effort in my not losing my good time. Hey, if you hadn't confessed, nothing would have happened at all...you ever think about that? And on top of all that, you get pretty grandiose with your confession...talking about marriage and that sort of stuff...stuff was entirely in "your" head...not in mine. You want to be sorry? Put the hundred bucks back on my books. You know, the fact that I had been saving that money over the months for Christmas, because my ex-S.O. spent my other funds, has me more pissed off that you could possibly imagine. That's being materialistic, I realize, but that's not against the law is it? That's me!! If you're feeling generous and in the Christmas spirit, you could always send more money. What I get will be spent on my kids and gas money to get to Golden. I'm having troubles with my Jeep on top of everything else and had to put it in the shop...Lord knows how I will pay for that but there wasn't any choice. I guess my point is that I have lots of problems at the moment. Myself, and most of them are of a financial sort. So loosening a hundred dollars was adding insult to injury. So much for my problems...that isn't the reason for writing to you.

I'd have to be awful stupid not to see that you think you're in love with me. For starters, Amber, you don't even know the real me. You've only come to know bits and pieces of who I am. There is so much more to me—you haven't a clue. So much more to me that I'm not sure you would like or understand...point remains—you do not know me. It's a good thing that you could not dig up my past because you would have been able to see through my act...my assertion. Remember life is but a play and we are all actors...the A&D program was merely a stage—do you see my point? Me—you and I—wrote our own scripts. Did I lie? By program standards (omission) probably. But in reality, or what we could call the "real world", no I did not! As far as I was concerned it wasn't program business. My choice! And my choices, most definitely, served me over time...but back on track. I was getting lost. Today I'm afraid to say that I love you too. It is a different "love" than what you, I assume, are feeling. I think you are a most intriguing person and I would love to have you as a friend...and maybe as a lover, but I am not "in love" with you. I refuse to lie to you! I'm not blind—it's obvious that you would take care of me forever...that you would do anything in the world for my love. I'm not sure what the future holds but I'm not going to take advantage of your infatuation, your love, your kindness, your compassion, your passion, your goodwill, etc. That's just not my style. Hopefully you already can see that. Honest, open, and willing to see what the future brings...does this mean I will return to Adams? It isn't a "yes" or "no", it's more a "maybe so"...I do not know that answer today. Like I tried to explain to you before, I have made some commitments to other people and I am a man of my "word", a man that you can respect and be proud of, a man you can count on when he gives his word, and to not fulfill those commitments would make me "less than" I would want to look in the mirror at, understand?

Now let's move on...

Please stop sending me program stuff! I hate that, enough is enough, I either got it or I didn't!! Choices [it would be nice if you let Paul make some]. Program is past tense. You can tell a person how to ride a bike until you are blue in the face, but they never really learn how to do it until you let them get on the bike and actually try, make sense? Thank you.

Cards! I love them! Rainbow trout, Mae West, Wizard of Oz, rainbows, flowers, sexual innuendos, I like them all. Some of the poems and passages were awesome, too. I like erotic cards too—like Olivia DeBarris or Michael Parkes, or even the unique or bizarre works of Escher. Check that stuff out and see what you think, Suryama? I'm not sure of the spelling on that last one, but you can find an example of the art in any month of Penthouse. Remember there are two sides of every coin. "Expression and impression"...these things can have both a negative and positive impact on the beholder...and the beauty in that is that it's their choice. Some people didn't like Monet either or understand Picasso, etc. Anyway, if you like sending me cards, well, I would be a liar if I said I didn't enjoy getting them. I've enjoyed every one of them—thanks!

I also enjoyed the pictures of you. Why the red hair of today? You looked good as a blonde in 1975. Now don't go out and change your hair color...I was just curious, that's all.

Well, it's Sunday and I'm going to put this in the mail. You need not send me twenty-two letters and cards in one day. I think we set some kind of record for the most mail in one day. Me cell mate is very envious. Several guys want your address but I wouldn't do such a thing to do...you sitting on my face sounded like a fun way to pass the night away.

The greatest help I could use is a substantial loan to get my Jeep back on the road. If you should consider this, keep in mind that my name is not Anderson and I would pay you back...Thanks!

Sincerely,

Paul

Rebuttal by Amber to Paul's Third Letter—Years Later

On Page Two of your letter number three, you admit that you love me, specifically Paragraph 2 of the letter. You say it's a different kind of love than my love for you. You say in your letter that am a most intriguing kind of person. I am a lot more of a person than what you describe me to be. I have changed a great deal since 1996. I am not the Mrs. Ferguson of yester year. I would even say [those are my initials now, and will be in the future] that you didn't know me in 1996 either. We were in an institutional setting, specifically a minimum security prison, where I was your counselor and you were my client. Makes a world of difference, doesn't it? I am a very busy person with little time on my hands. I recently restored my 1898 European Farm House Style House that I bought in 1996. I have cork floors in the kitchen and living room. I haven't touched my 1898 tongue and groove cedar that's on the second and third floors. The first floor walls have been painted marmalade, lime and creamy white. You don't even have to go to Hawaii. It's a tropical paradise, right here at home. The home feels new to me. I really enjoy the country feeling to the home, with having two lots. The trees are beautiful. I have three apricot trees, a blue spruce, a Siberian elm, and an American elm. The home was built by Charles Boock, a German immigrant. The stone base was actually built by two sons who were stone masons. The home was the original cigar factory house and operated as a cigar factory until the 1920s. Mrs. Nellis restored the home in the 1980's. The home had sat empty for 12 years. Mrs. Nellis is 101 years old and lives in Dillon, Montana. I recently visited her and she is an awesome lady. I traveled to Ketchum and Stanley, Idaho where I took my award winning shot, "A Final Destination." The old trucks were gone but I actually have a little bit of history in that photograph. In addition, I went to Salmon, Idaho, which is the fly fishing capital of the world. I remember you telling me that you like to fly fish. My favorite places were Salmon, Idaho and Dillon, Montana. I still like Roseburg, Colorado and would like to have a home in Glide on the North Umpqua River. Well, I really got off the subject didn't I? Sorry about that.

In your third letter to me, you said you would love to have me as a friend. What happened to that suggestion, Paul? That would be a nice place to start and catch up on things... After all it's been twenty years since I saw you in the flesh. You also said that you would maybe take me as your lover. That is a bit of a stretch if I say so myself... Friendship would be the place I would like to start as you said in your letter. To suggest lover is a big assumption! You said in your letter that you were not in love with me I feel the same way. I am not in love with you. Actually, I have been with someone for twenty years. Ron has been my rock, someone who is honest, dependable and trustworthy. He's created a lot of security to me throughout those twenty years. You said in your letter that you refused to lie to me. I can't stand a liar person. I am glad that you're not blind. Me neither. Let's discuss these topics in the future at some point in time. I am a very busy person as I am sure you are too. I wouldn't ever want to take care of you. I don't care for or take care of needy persons, point blank...I would take care of you if you were sick and we were in a committed relationship. That's an entirely different story. As you say in your letter, who knows what the future will bring. I wouldn't take advantage of you. I am a very independent person and very able to take care of myself without someone leaning on my shoulder. You talk about infatuation in your letter. Sounds like a girl school crush or something. I was in my forties when I met you. I think it had to be more than a crush Paul...I am still a kind person, but less naïve and more realistic these days. I am still passionate but limit my passions to half a dozen things. I am more focused and driven these days. Life is very short, so I like enjoying my passions with only certain people in my life. Life is to be enjoyed. I will be doing extensive traveling in the future. Lots of places and people to see. I remember you asking me if you could go to Hawaii with me. I would like that very much, Paul. I went to Hawaii in 2006, traveling to Kauai. That's a long story and I will save it for a time when we get together. You told me who you were in your letters to me, especially your third letter. You said you were honest, open, and willing to see what the future brings. I agree with those feelings too. Let's see what happens when we get together.

Fourth Letter—Last Letter From Paul—December 9, 1996

Amber,

This is going to be the last letter that you will probably ever get from me. I'm not much of a letter writer on the streets. I'm usually too busy to pick up a pen...even sending Christmas cards will be something new for me. I suppose I owe you a thank you for all the cards and attention. Thanks.

I'm not sure if I will be going to Adams in the future...maybe and maybe not...My girlfriend says she's not going to let me get away. I'm not entirely sold on that idea either...15 years of being married is enough to cure any man. Especially after a woman walks out. I don't think anyone is going to get their hooks into me...I need some breathing room in order to figure out what or where I'm headed. Time to sift through my options. I'm sure you understand what I'm trying to convey to you...as you said, space...

You wrote and said that you would honor my wishes. That means that you will not be outside Colorado Territorial Correctional Facility on the 17th. My girlfriend and an old partner will be here to take me home...I do not wish to go through any B.S. in the parking lot of this place, which wouldn't be to your advantage. I certainly would not be interested in going to Adams after something like that. Being here is not going to change my mind...believe that, so cool your jets. You never know what the future will hold.

Thank you for sending the money to pay the fine...that's very honorable of you. If we were in opposite situations, I would have done the same. As far as a loan for repairs to my Jeep...well it's supposed to go in the shop this week—so I don't know how bad it is going to be yet. You're not obligated to help me but it certainly would be appreciated. I would only accept your help if there are no strings attached.

I just got some more cards from you...You don't seem to getting the idea...do not show up here! This is crazy. You're starting to make me worry. Kind of like that movie *Misery*. You're being very domineering. That does not work for me. You're in love with your ideas not me. Shakespeare says that the whole world is but a stage and we are actors and actresses...I'd rather be a director. That requires being able to make my own choices. Relationships require interaction between two or more people. So far, in the picture you have drawn for me, I see myself as a puppet...choices, no interaction, less than human...

So it's my belief that it would never work at this rate. I could be wrong! Convince me by showing some restraint. Please do not show up for my release— this would be a good start for our friendship

Thanks for everything,
Happy Holidays,
Paul

Rebuttal to Fourth Letter—Discussion

Paul, once again, thanks Amber for the cards she sent him. An interesting point Paul makes is that he says that nobody will not get their hooks into him. Going back in time, there was a discussion with another inmate. I asked this inmate "What does it mean when you have hooked a man?" He answered by saying "Now that you have hooked him, you need to reel him in."

Paul holds out a carrot to Amber by saying, "You never know what the future will bring." Paul is protesting that he was married for fifteen years and that he's not entirely sold on the idea of marriage again. He says that he needs breathing room in order to figure out what or where he's headed. Paul says he needs time to sift through his options. In the last sentence in paragraph two, he talks to Amber about how she understands what he is conveying to her, with a reference to a word she used in a letter to Paul: "as you said, space."

Paul is very strong in his request that Amber not show up at Colorado Territorial Correctional Facility on December 17th for his release dat. He doesn't want any B.S. in the parking lot. If Amber shows up, he wouldn't be interested in going to Adams after something like that.

Thanks Amber for sending him money to pay for his fine. He tells her that it was very honorable of her. He says that if their positions were opposite, he would do the same for her. He talks once again about his Jeep having to go into the shop for repairs. He doesn't know how much it's going to cost. Paul tells Amber that she's not obligated to help but it certainly would be appreciated. Paul uses the word loan when asking for Amber's help.

Paul receives more cards from Amber. He tells her she isn't getting the idea of showing up here! Paul tells her she is being very domineering and that she is making him start to worry. Paul tells Amber that being domineering doesn't work for him. He tells her that she's in love with her ideas, not him. Paul even quotes Shakespeare by saying that we are actors and actresses on stage...that he wants to be a director...that requires him to make his own choices. Relationships require interaction between two or more people. Paul tells Amber that the picture she has drawn for him is one of no choices and that he sees himself as a puppet...no choices, no interaction...less than human...

Paul closes his letter to Amber by saying that it is his belief that it would never work out at this rate. But then he tells Amber that he could be wrong! He tells her to show some restraint and not show up for his release—this would be a good start to our friendship.

Thanks for everything,
Happy Holidays,
Paul

Afterward— During the week of December 17th, Amber travels to Canon City with a friend. She stays the night there at the Marriott Hotel. She finds in her bag a court docket number for Paul's trial whereby he was sentenced to prison. Upon arriving in Canon City, they drive around for a while and eventually have lunch at a local restaurant. After that, they arrive at C.T.C.F. and stop at the turnaround in front of the main entrance. However, Amber does show restraint and does not go inside. After not seeing Paul come out of the main entrance, Amber leaves and headed back to Adams.

Chapter 6

"Release Date—December 17, 1996 From Colorado Territorial Correctional Facility, Canon City, Colorado"

Release Date—Sunday, December 17, 1996—Freedom

The statewide population of persons incarcerated in Colorado in 1996 is approximately 12,000. From 1995 to 2001 Dave Cook is the Director of the Department of Corrections. S. Frank Thompson was the Superintendent for the Department of Corrections. This information came from the Bureau of Justice Statistics. Patterson was discharged fully and completed post-prison supervision in 1999. He lived after his release from prison in various cities throughout Colorado and California.

On September 30, 1999, nearly four years from his release date of December 17, 1996, he married again. They were married in Denver, Colorado. Paul's parents' names Edwen and Florance Patterson.

Chapter 7

"Letters Never Sent to Paul from Amber"

Letters Never Sent After Release Date

Paul,

I am willing to wait, no matter how long it takes. No one can measure up to you. All I want is you. I would climb the highest mountain for you...

Amber

Paul, give us a shot. Can I have a second chance? We have so much in common.

Love is about learning. Listen, observe, and just be.

--Written in 2000

Time has put some distance between us. Even so, I can still feel hurt when remembering those events nearly four years ago. The pain is fresh as a new wound. For instance, I get caught up on old thoughts and feelings. I talked to an old client today. He brought me back to remembering the past. What in fact is old stuff? He told me I was a good counselor. I have grown older and wiser the last two years because of the experiences and knowledge I have gained by being a caregiver to so many people. But the pain of the past is still present. I ask myself, will it ever go away? The reality is the pain. Do I enjoy feeling this way? I think back to when you enclosed a slip with the word Eternity on it, the name of my favorite scent. Do you know that Eternity means a long period of time that seems endless...that's what I am feeling today. Will I ever see you again? I hope it's not in another life time...

March 27, 2011
4:00 A.M.

Loosen up! I have no expectations of you! Now or never...Eternity—remember that one. My favorite perfume. I give it as a gift to my best friends now.

John Carey said once that if you wanted to take care of people, you should be a caregiver! He's in Arizona. What a...he gave me, prior to my departure from Colorado State Penitentiary, the last job review.

I had the best boundaries of any counselor there. I guess things went to the wayside fast...oh well. After my release/termination from Colorado State Penitentiary, I had to fight for unemployment, got an attorney from Denver, and won my case. John C. was on the other phone and was stuttering. I loved it. We were so organized.

I have been a caregiver since March of 1998, although my hat is always on it seems. Wages for the state and most private pay sucks. My best friend Kathy got me my current job, which I have been at since May 7th, 2008! I want to stay, but mostly if her son doesn't declare my grandmother is from Switzerland, Germany, or Australia/New Zealand. My mom turns 97 in October.

I love to travel. My Hawaiian looks will start with Makai (bad spelling). Kauai will be in the middle. I was a social worker in a grade school at the hottest little place on the island of Kauai in 2006. Kauai has changed so much, it's said. There is a place there with stars and celebrities. Very expensive. Did you ever make it to Hawaii?

Congratulations on your marriage. I didn't say so earlier in my letters. How long have you and your wife been married?

I am totally focused these days. No distractions. Everything can be a distraction.

Dick and I divorced in 1998. He remarried shortly after (9 months) to Nancy, a Kentucky sweetheart. He doesn't let her out of his sight. It is funny, he acts like a body guard. It's really funny...funny to her, not me. I loved that home, actually. I have loved all of my homes.

The Boock house is my favorite; however it has a lot of charm. 1200 square feet, almost.

Last thing that happened to me. Going through my exit—stage door left/right was interesting. I am glad I didn't have to do that in real time again. No one gives a darn, never to talk to me or see me again—ex-communication!

Paul you are the only man/friend I have ever been intimate with ever. Do you understand? Webster Dictionary's definition. It doesn't have to do with sex, that's a different level. If you have that intimacy with friends, it's truly remarkable. I am very happy for you and only wish you the best in everything.

I have sent you basically four letters, several times. I truly understand where you were coming from in 1996. Have you tried writing? You are an excellent writer. Photography? What are you shooting these days? Most recently, I went to Fossil, OR and stayed at Wilson's B&B and shot the Painted Hills again. It was wonderful at Wilson's and the Painted Hills were gorgeous.

Chapter 8

"June 10, 2010—Paul Returns to Adams"

Paul,

Change, believe it, see it, and achieve it. I hope these words offer you some encouragement...

> Love,
> Amber

Paul,

Be vulnerable, tell everything. Do less, do more. Eat and enjoy. I miss everything about you...

> Love,
> Amber

These letters were really therapeutic to Amber. She still feels connected to Paul even though the letters were never sent. They provided hope and encouragement to Amber, too.

June 10, 2010—14 ½ Years After Paul's Release Date

I am working at Anna's home. I will stay the night with her. I started my shift at 4 o'clock. After Sherry left for the day, I began fixing dinner. We would be having barbeque chicken with Sherry's homemade barbeque sauce that was simply delicious. Sherry and Anna had gone to Boulder today to get fresh fruit and vegetables. It gave Anna a nice outing for the day and she could talk about growing up in Boulder. After eating dinner, Anna liked to look at the evening newspaper. What followed was her regular routine of watching Jeopardy and Wheel of Fortune, her two favorite shows on television. I finished cleaning up and sat down to take a chance at the newspaper. There was a section of photographs taken at the annual motorcycle rally. I turned the page to look at the photographs. I couldn't believe my eyes. Were my eyes playing tricks on me? In front of me, there was Paul in one of the photographs. I was really surprised to see his photograph. Actually, I couldn't believe my eyes. That's what I said to myself. He hadn't changed and looked really good!! Not only was the photograph striking, but so was the motorcycle. It looked expensive and the chrome was polished and shined with the sun's rays on it. Yes, it was him alright. He actually returned to Adams after all these years. I cut out the photograph form the newspaper as Anna rarely looked at the newspaper again. I tucked the paper into my bag to bring home with me. I would remember this day forever...

March 27, 2011—Letter sent to Paul in response to seeing his photograph in the local Democrat-Herald newspaper

Paul,

How have you been? I saw your photograph in the Democrat-Herald in June of last year. You look really good and haven't changed a whole lot. What have you been doing these days? Where are you working? Your motorcycle is sure nice. Do you ride it a lot? I've enclosed a slip of paper with my telephone number on it. Hope you will call sometime.

I have a really good job taking care of a lady who lives in Adams. Actually, I have been taking care of people since 1997. This is the best paying job I have ever had. Even better than a counselor.

My address is also enclosed, if you are ever back in Adams or wish to write me.

Take care,

Amber

P.S. It was good seeing you, if only in a photograph...

So Much Better With Time. If it's real love, it always come back to you.

In 2016, Amber had the photograph that appeared in the newspaper blown up to an 8x10 photograph. It showed a lot more detail and revealed something. Paul had placed on one of his handlebars of the motorcycle an apple. Amber went to the Adams County public library to do research on what it meant by the word "apple." In the reference room, she located a book on phrases. In that book, she found the meaning of an apple. An apple's meaning is this: the apple of [someone's eye, a favorite, a person who is greatly loved by someone]... She found this out on March 23, 2016, at the same library that Paul had worked at on a work crew while in prison in 1996...

So Much Better With Time. If it's real love, it always come back to you...

"Storms make oaks take roots."

A Proverb

THE END

www.ingramcontent.com/pod-product-compliance
Lightning Source LLC
Chambersburg PA
CBHW051957090426
42741CB00008B/1439